LEARN
BRIDGE IN
A WEEKEND

LEARN
BRIDGE IN
A WEEKEND

JONATHAN DAVIS
Foreword by ZIA MAHMOOD

Photography by Matthew Ward

DORLING KINDERSLEY
London • New York • Stuttgart

A DORLING KINDERSLEY BOOK

Designer Emma Boys
Editor Tony Mudd
Senior Art Editor Mandy Lunn
Deputy Art Director Tina Vaughan
Deputy Editorial Director Jane Laing
Production Controller Helen Creeke

First published in Great Britain in 1993
by Dorling Kindersley Limited,
9 Henrietta Street, London WC2E 8PS

Reprinted 1994

A CIP catalogue record for this book is available from the British Library

ISBN 0-75130-060-8

Computer page make-up by Cloud 9 Designs
Reproduced by Colourscan, Singapore
Printed and bound by Arnoldo Mondadori, Verona, Italy

CONTENTS

Foreword 6

PREPARING FOR THE WEEKEND 8

THE WEEKEND COURSE 22

Day 1

Day 2

AFTER THE WEEKEND 80

FOREWORD

·

BRIDGE IS WITHOUT QUESTION the most stimulating card
game ever invented. That is one reason why an estimated 100
million people play in 50 countries around the world. The other
is that the game is simply irresistible. Few who make the effort
to learn the game ever give it up. In 15 years of playing the game,
I can honestly say that I have been endlessly fascinated. Bridge
is a game of almost infinite beauty. The more you play, the more
you become enthralled. Yet many people miss out entirely on
the experience because they think that learning the game
would prove too difficult. Believe me when I say

JONATHAN DAVIS

the hardest part is not learning how to play. It is deciding that
you want to try. This book is designed to help you overcome
that fear of putting your first foot in the water. The first section,
entitled Preparing for the Weekend, outlines the basic rules of
the game to get you started, and the Weekend Course itself builds
on the basics to teach you many of the tactics and techniques you
need to understand and play the game. The emphasis throughout
is on common sense natural bidding – something of which I approve.
Your reward for making the effort to learn bridge is that, like millions
before, you will experience the pleasure and satisfaction that bridge
brings, whether you play simply for amusement, or as a serious sport.
Come on in – the water is warm.

ZIA MAHMOOD
Zia first came to prominence
as one of the Pakistan team
which reached the world team
championships' final in 1981.
Since then he has won many top
tournaments around the world,
and plays high-stakes rubber
bridge in London and New York.

PREPARING FOR THE WEEKEND

Learning about the cards and their values

BRIDGE IS A GAME FOR FOUR PEOPLE who play in two opposing pairs. This course, however, is designed for you to learn on your own. All the equipment you need is a standard pack of 52 playing cards, so you can play through the examples. If you are unused to card games, begin by familiarizing yourself with the four suits of the standard pack – spades ♠, hearts ♥, diamonds ♦, and clubs ♣ – and with the 13 cards in each suit. Even if, like most people, you are already familiar with the pack, you need to learn how the suits and individual cards are valued in a game of bridge.

SUITS AND RANK

In bridge, the four suits are not equal. They are ranked in the following order: spades (the highest), hearts, diamonds, and clubs (the lowest). It is best to memorize the ranking order of the suits before you proceed any further, because it plays an important part in the game.

MAJORS AND MINORS
The two higher-ranking suits, spades and hearts, are called the major suits. Diamonds and clubs are known as the minor suits. They are worth less points in the scoring.

CARD VALUES
The Ace is the highest value card in each suit, and the Two is the lowest. Here the cards of each suit are fanned out in order of value, with the highest positioned on the left and the lowest on the right.

PLAYING HANDS

All 52 cards in the pack are used in bridge. To start the game each of the four players is dealt 13 cards. Those 13 cards make up a player's hand. Each time the cards are dealt, all four players take part in a process known as the bidding. This results in one side undertaking to win a certain number of the 13 possible tricks and the other side trying to stop them doing so. Tricks and contracts are further explained p.13. The object of the game is to score more points than the other side over a succession of deals, known as a **rubber**.

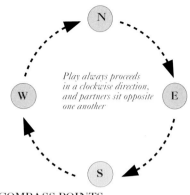

Play always proceeds in a clockwise direction, and partners sit opposite one another

COMPASS POINTS
The examples in this book follow the convention of labelling bridge partners as North/South (N/S) and East/West (E/W).

HONOUR CARDS

The five top cards in each suit, the Ace, King, Queen, Jack, and Ten, are known as **honours**. They are the most powerful cards in each suit. The Ace, King, Queen, and Jack are also known as high cards. You will use a simple point-count system (see below) to value your high cards when you are learning to bid (see pp.24-25).

The Ace is the • top card in each suit. Count 4 points for each one you hold

The King is • the second highest card. Count 3 points for each King

• Count 2 high-card points for each Queen

• Count 1 high-card point for each Jack, sometimes known as the Knave

• Although the Ten is an **honour** card, it does not qualify for a high-card point value

PREPARING TO PLAY

Cutting for partners, shuffling, cutting, and dealing the cards

•

BEFORE YOU START to play bridge, there are certain preliminaries to carry out. Over the years, bridge players have developed a routine for deciding who partners whom, who sits where, and who deals the first hand. There are also rules governing how the cards are shuffled, cut, and dealt. Each of the four players has a role to play. It is customary to play bridge with two packs of cards, alternating them between deals. Once the cards have been dealt, you need to know how to sort your hand sensibly, so that you can recognize at a glance what cards you are holding in each of the four suits.

CHOOSING PARTNERS

Each player picks a card from the pack spread out face-down on the table. The two players who draw the highest cards play together against the other two. These partnerships continue until the end of the **rubber** (see p.21). The player with the highest card chooses where to sit and also deals the first hand.

PAIRING
If players draw cards of equal value, the ranking of the suit decides which is higher. So, if these four cards (left) were drawn, the player with the Jack would partner the player with ♥6, as hearts are of a higher rank than diamonds.

PREPARING TO DEAL
The dealer's left-hand opponent, West, shuffles the cards, and passes them across the table to his partner, East, who cuts the pack into two piles. The dealer, South, completes the cut by placing the bottom pile onto the top pile. She is then ready to deal. Meanwhile, the dealer's partner, North, shuffles the spare pack ready for the next deal.

North

East

• *The player on the dealer's right cuts the cards into two piles*

West

South Dealer

SHUFFLING

There are two ways to shuffle the cards, the hand-over-hand shuffle (right) and the riffle (below). Both require a little practice, but the hand-over-hand shuffle is marginally easier. Whichever method you use, the aim is to ensure that the cards are thoroughly reordered before being dealt.

RIFFLE
Hold half the cards in each hand, and bend the corners up (below). Spray the overlapping edges together. Push the two halves together.

HAND OVER HAND
Split the pack and lift one half above the other. Drop cards into the middle and to either side of those in your lower hand several times.

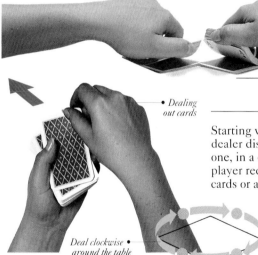

• Dealing out cards

Deal clockwise • around the table

DEALING

Starting with the player on her left, the dealer distributes all 52 cards, one by one, in a clockwise direction. If a player receives the wrong number of cards or a card is exposed during the deal, she must deal again. After each hand has been played, the deal passes to the player on the previous dealer's left.

SORTING

When you pick up your cards, sort them into alternate red and black suits, and arrange the cards within each suit by value, from the highest on the left to the lowest on the right. This will make it easy for you to see at a glance how many cards you have in each suit, and how powerful the cards are. Be careful to hold your cards up and away from the table. They should be concealed from your opponents, and also from your partner, at all times.

THE BASICS

*From bidding to winning the **rubber***

EACH HAND, OR DEAL, in bridge falls into two parts. The first is the bidding, which takes the form of an **auction**. This establishes which side is prepared to try to make the most tricks on that deal – known as the contract. The second part in bridge is the play of the cards. By playing all 52 cards as 13 tricks, you discover whether the side that bid the contract can make as many tricks as it has said it can. This in turn determines which side will score points on the hand.

BIDDING

Understanding the principles of bidding

BIDDING AUCTION

The bidding starts as soon as the cards have been dealt. The dealer is the first player to have the chance to bid, followed by the player on his left and so on round the table in a clockwise direction. Nobody is required to bid. You can always say "No bid" or "Pass". But if you do bid, you must make a higher ranking bid than anything that has gone before. It makes sense to bid only if you think that your side has a good chance of winning more tricks than your opponents. The minimum number of tricks you can bid to make is seven out of the possible 13 that can be won. The maximum number of tricks you can bid is 13.

RANKING OF BIDS

Suits rank in the order shown here, with spades the highest and clubs the lowest. Bids follow suit, so a bid of One spade is higher than that of One heart. A bid of One No Trump is higher than any suit bid at the "One Level".

HAND NOTATION

For ease and speed of understanding, the cards in a player's hand are usually indicated in annotated form (right). The suits are always shown in ranking order, with the highest-ranking suit – spades – at the top and the lowest-ranking suit – clubs – at the bottom. The example shown here represents the hand of cards shown on page 11.

♠ A J 10
♥ K J 5 2
♦ Q 5 2
♣ J 10 7

LEVELS OF BID

The rules of bridge lay down how and what you are allowed bid. Bids must be made in a standardized form, consisting of a number from one to seven and one of five possible denominations: No Trumps, spades, hearts, diamonds, or clubs. The number refers to the number of tricks *above six* that you think your side can win. So, for example, a bid of One heart (1♥) is a bid (at the One Level) to make seven tricks (6+1=7) with hearts as the trump suit. The highest bid that you can make is Seven No Trumps (7NT), a bid (at the Seven Level) to make thirteen tricks (6+7=13) without a trump suit.

YOUR PARTNER

Bidding sounds complicated, but the basic principle is very simple. Your aim is to work out how many tricks your side can make – and to pick the denomination (suit or No Trumps) that gives you the best chance of making the most tricks. The skill lies in the fact that you must find the right answer without being able to see any of the other players' hands. The bids you make are the only method you have to give information about your hand to your partner. So, to do well in bridge, you must learn to conduct a dialogue with your partner through the bids you make. However, that does not mean, as many people think, that you must learn a complex or difficult bidding system.

With hearts as trumps, ♥3 wins this trick

With everyone able to follow suit, ♠K wins this trick

TRUMP OR NO TRUMP

The concept of trumps or No Trumps is fundamental in bridge. With most hands, the bidding will end with one of the four suits being named as the trump suit. During the play in that hand cards from the trump suit will outrank all the other cards in all the other suits. If, for instance, hearts are chosen as trumps, and your opponents play the Ace of diamonds (♦A), if you do not have a diamond in your hand, you can play a card from your trump suit. This card, whether it be the two or the Ace, will rank higher than the diamonds and so win the trick. Trumps are potentially very powerful, and you will usually try to discover your and your partner's longest combined suit and name it as trumps.

WINNING TRICKS
Each player plays a card in turn. You must follow suit, if you can. Otherwise, you must either play a trump, or **discard** a card from another suit. Once all four players have played a card this constitutes a trick. The trick is won by whoever plays the highest-ranked card. In No Trumps that means the highest card in the suit that was led first. In a trump contract the winning card may be a trump. The trick is then credited to the partnership of the player who played the winning card.

SCORING SYSTEM
The key thing to grasp is that the scoring rewards you for bidding accurately. On most deals you want to aim to bid the maximum number of tricks that your side can make. At the end of each hand the scores are entered on the scorecard. Your side gets a plus score every time you make a contract you have bid. But if you win fewer tricks than you predicted, your opponents score.

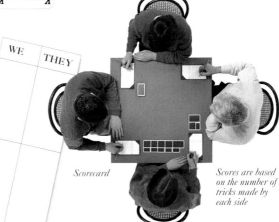

Scorecard

Scores are based on the number of tricks made by each side

TRUMP CONTRACT

How to find out if you have a good suit fit

OPENING THE BIDDING

Suppose you, as South, have dealt the cards shown right. Do you open the bidding or say No bid? Your hand has two Aces, one King, two Queens, and one Jack. Using the high-card point system (see p.9) you have 16 of the 40 points in the pack. With so many high cards, the odds favour your side being able to make over half the tricks. So you certainly want to bid.

♠ J 10 6 2
♥ 10 5
♦ 9 5 4 2
♣ K 9 5

♠ K 9   ♠ A 8 7 3
♥ K 9 4   ♥ 8 6
♦ Q 8 6 3   ♦ J 10 7
♣ Q 10 7 3   ♣ A J 6 4

♠ Q 5 4
♥ A Q J 7 3 2
♦ A K
♣ 8 2

West   *North*   *East*

South

WHAT TO BID

Your hand has six hearts, three spades, two diamonds, and two clubs. Common sense suggests that you will make the most tricks if hearts, your longest suit, is chosen as trumps. So your first bid will be in hearts – but at what level? With all but the very strongest hands it is generally best to open the bidding at the One Level and wait to hear what your partner has to say in response. So on this hand you will bid One heart. The standard rule of thumb is: you should open the bidding with 13 high-card points or more.

— THE RULES AND TERMS OF BIDDING —

Here is a summary of the main rules of bidding for ready reference:

BIDDING OPTIONS
• Bids must either name a suit as trumps, or specify No Trumps, e.g. 1♥ (One heart), or 1NT (One No Trump).
• If you do not wish to bid because you do not have a strong enough hand, you must say "No bid" or "**Pass**".
• A player may also say "**double**". This bid is explained on page 21.

VALID BIDS
• As in any **auction**, to be valid a bid must outrank all earlier bids.
• The lowest bid you can make is at the "One Level" (1NT, 1♠, 1♥, 1♦, 1♣). This

is a bid to make the minimum number of seven tricks.
• A valid bid cannot be retracted.

BID RANKINGS
• Bids rank in suit order: spades (the highest), then hearts, diamonds, and clubs (the lowest). For example, a bid of 1♠ outranks a bid of 1♥, which outranks a bid of 1♦, which in turn outranks 1♣.
• No Trump bids rank above suit bids at the same level. So a bid of 1NT outranks 1♠; and a bid of 2NT outranks 2♥.

FINAL BID
• The bidding comes to an end when a bid is followed by three consecutive "No bids". The final bid then becomes the contract.

BIDDING AUCTION

Your chance to bid does not always end when you have made one bid. In fact, the bidding can go round the table several times. It only stops when three players in succession have **passed** (or said No bid). The last bid to be made – which by definition is also the highest, as any bid must be higher than the one before to be valid – sets the final contract. On some hands you may find yourself bidding three or four times before the bidding auction is finally over. The art of bidding lies in working out from your own hand and the bids called by the other players how many tricks your side can expect to make.

♠ Q 10 4 2
♥ K J 3
♦ 10 8
♣ J 6 5 4

♠ 9 5		♠ 7
♥ 8 7 6 4	N	♥ A 10 9 2
♦ Q J 4	W E	♦ 9 5 3 2
♣ K Q 10 8	S	♣ A 9 3 2

♠ A K J 8 6 3
♥ Q 5
♦ A K 7 6
♣ 7

SOUTH	WEST	NORTH	EAST
1♠	Pass	2♠	Pass
4♠	Pass	Pass	Pass

UNDERSTANDING THE BID

In this example, South deals and opens the bidding. She bids 1♠, naming her longest suit. The comments below show how all four players might look at their hands and bid.

NORTH

I have only a few high cards – one King, one Queen, two Jacks, a total of seven points. But I do have four spades, the suit my partner bid. I am just strong enough to bid 2♠, a simple raise in her suit. With more high cards I might bid higher in spades. With a weaker hand (0-5 points) I would **pass**.

♠ Q 10 4 2
♥ K J 3
♦ 10 8
♣ J 6 5 4

EAST

I have two obvious winners – the two Aces, 8 points – but the rest of my hand is mediocre. By the time the bidding reaches me, North has bid 2♠, and to bid a suit I would have to bid at the Three Level, promising to make nine tricks – out of the question with this below-average hand.

♠ 7
♥ A 10 9 2
♦ 9 5 3 2
♣ A 9 3 2

♠ 9 5
♥ 8 7 6 4
♦ Q J 4
♣ K Q 10 8

WEST

I have only 8 points – one King, two Queens, and a Jack – and no long suit to bid. So I must **pass**. To bid over South's 1♠, which is the highest ranking suit, I would have to call 1NT or Two of a suit. My hand is not nearly strong enough to risk doing that. However, if my partner can bid, I may rethink.

SOUTH

My 1♠ showed I had an above-average hand and a four-card spade suit. In fact, I have 17 high-card points and a good six-card suit – which is more than the minimum I could have to open the bidding. So when North bids 2♠, I can afford to bid again at a higher level. I shall go for ten tricks by bidding 4♠ at my second turn.

♠ A K J 8 6 3
♥ Q 5
♦ A K 7 6
♣ 7

NO TRUMP CONTRACT

How to find out if No Trumps is the best option

BIDDING ACCURATELY

By now you should have a sense of how the bidding process works and the important role that bids can play in sending messages to partners. Bridge is a partnership game and unless you can learn to communicate with your partner, in both bidding and play, you will not get far. The art of good bidding lies in trying to work out how many tricks you think your side can make based not just on what is in your hand but on what you can deduce about the cards that your partner holds. The combined strength of your two hands is what you are trying to assess. Hands in bridge fall into two main types – those where only one side is making bids and those where both sides are competing against each other for the right to name the contract. The second type is known as a contested auction. Most contested auctions end in a trump contract by one side or the other.

North hand:
♠ AK 7 6
♥ 10 9 2
♦ K 6
♣ A 9 4 3

West hand:
♠ 10 8 5 4
♥ A 7 5
♦ Q 10 9 3
♣ J 10

East hand:
♠ Q J 2
♥ K 8 6 4
♦ 5 4
♣ 8 7 6 5

South hand:
♠ 9 3
♥ Q J 3
♦ A J 8 7 2
♣ K Q 2

SOUTH	WEST	NORTH	EAST
1♦	Pass	1♠	Pass
1NT	Pass	3NT	Pass

UNDERSTANDING THE BID

Here is another example of how a typical bridge hand might be bid. When you and your partner have strength in all four suits, and no long combined suit that you want to name as trumps, you may decide to opt for a contract in No Trumps instead. South makes the opening bid, 1♦. Her partner's first bid – known as a response – is 1♠. South's second bid – or rebid in bridge terminology – is 1NT. North's bid of 3NT completes the bidding. East and West **pass** throughout.

NORTH – 1ST BID
My partner has opened the bidding with 1♦. I have two Aces and two Kings, an above average hand, so I do not want to pass. If I bid 1♠ I show I have a spade suit and suggest that as trumps.

NORTH – 2ND BID
My partner has rebid in No Trumps. She cannot support my spades. We do not have a trump **fit**, so No Trumps looks best. I can raise to 3NT to show my strength.

SOUTH – 2ND BID
My 1♦ bid showed an above average hand with a diamond suit. I cannot support spades, so I bid 1NT to show an all-round but minimum opening hand.

SOUTH – 3RD BID
I shall **pass** 3NT. I have shown the strength and shape of my hand with my two previous bids. I have no reason to bid again, so I shall pass.

KEY BIDDING FACTORS

Essential factors to bear in mind during the bidding

HOW HIGH TO BID

The three factors that determine how high your side should bid are: the combined high-card strength of the two hands, whether or not you have a good trump fit, and what you stand to score for the different types of bid you are considering. In general, the higher you bid, the greater the potential score you stand to make (see pp.20-21). There are 35 contracts your side can bid, from 1♣ to 7NT.

FINDING A GOOD FIT

These examples show that a great deal of bidding revolves around two simple questions: how high should our side bid? And should we bid in trumps or No Trumps? If you and your partner have eight or more cards in a suit between you, you know you have the clear majority of the cards in that suit – and that you will normally make the most tricks by naming that suit as trumps when you bid. You have found a good trump fit.

BIDDING SYSTEMS

Experts have developed many bidding systems over the years. Do you have to learn one in order to play bridge? No. As a beginner, you cannot avoid learning a few basic rules and precepts. You will need to learn how to use the point-count system to value your hand, for example (see pp.24-25), and also the different types of opening bids and responses. But you certainly do not need to memorize a string of complex bidding rules before you sit down to play. Be warned though that bidding habits do tend to vary quite considerably from country to country – and even within countries. The bidding summary (see pp.90-91) gives you an outline of the two most popular natural bidding systems, **Standard American** and **Acol**.

ELY CULBERTSON
American bridge expert Ely Culbertson was the first to develop and market a comprehensive natural bidding system. Some of his ideas survive to this day.

PLAYING THE CARDS

An introduction to winning tricks

♠ A 10 6 2
♥ 8 4
♦ A 6 2
♣ A Q 8 7

♠ 8 7 4
♥ Q J 5 2
♦ Q J 8 3
♣ 5 4

N
W   E
S

♠ 3
♥ A K 10 9 7 3
♦ 10 9 7
♣ K 6 3

♠ K Q J 9 5
♥ 6
♦ K 5 4
♣ J 10 9 2

SOUTH	WEST	NORTH	EAST
Pass	Pass	1♣	1♥
1♠	2♥	2♠	3♥
4♠	Pass	Pass	Pass

A SAMPLE HAND

Now you know the basics of bidding, you are ready to see how a hand is played. In this example, both sides have decided to compete in the bidding – something that happens often in bridge when both sides have long combined holdings in a suit that they can name as trumps. Despite being outnumbered in high cards, East and West have ten hearts between them and can bid "Three hearts" without any great risk. This is not enough however to stop South outbidding them with "Four spades". This is a contract to make ten tricks.

BEGINNING PLAY

Because South was the first player to have bid the suit of the contract (her 1♠ bid), she becomes the "declarer" and must play the contract. The first card is always led by the player to the declarer's left – one of the declarer's opponents, the "defenders" against the contract. In this case, West leads ♥2. He knows from the bidding that East is strong in hearts, and hopes his partner can win the trick.

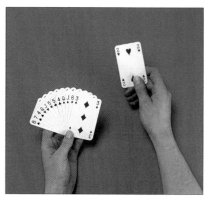

THE DUMMY

After West has made the opening lead, North places his hand face-up on the table with the trump suit to his far right (in No Trumps, the suits can be arranged in any order). This hand is called the dummy. North will take no further part in the play of the hand. From now on it is up to South, as the declarer, to play both her cards and those of the dummy.

THE FIRST TRICK

Once the dummy has been put down, the play continues in a clockwise direction around the table, with each person playing a card in turn. The declarer (South) plays a card, ♥4, from the dummy (North) and then East plays ♥K. Whoever plays the highest-ranking card wins the trick, and then goes on to play the first card to the next trick. Here East's ♥K wins the trick as South's only heart is the six. When tricks are displayed as cards (as below), South's card always appears vertically and centrally at the southernmost position in the pile.

MISSING ACE
When East plays ♥K, she knows that South cannot beat it, as East holds the only higher heart (♥A) herself.

TRICK 2 •
East leads her ♥A. It does not win the trick as South trumps it with the ♠5. South can do this as she has no more hearts with which to follow suit.

TRICK 3 •
South's trump won the second trick. Now she leads a top trump (♠K). Everyone follows suit. South is trying to **draw** all the opponents' trumps.

TRICK 4 •
South wins and leads trumps again, continuing the attempt to exhaust the opponents' trumps. East has no trumps left and so **discards** ♥3.

1	2	3	4	5	6	7	8	9	10	11	12	13	
W	E	S	S	N	S	E	N	N	N	S	S	S	
♥2	♥A	♠K	♠9	♠6	♣J	♦10	♠A	♠Q	♠8	♠J	♦K	♦5	
N	S	W	W	E	W	S	E	E	W				
♥4	♠5	♠4	♠7	♥7	♣4	♦4	♠3	♣6	♥9	♥Q			*Lead •*
E	W	N	N	S	N	W	S	S					
♥K	♥5	♠2	♠A	♠Q	♣7	♦3	♣2	♣9					• *N/S win*
S	N	E	E	W	E	N	W						
♥6	♥8	♣3	♥3	♣8	♣K	♦A	♣5						• *E/W win*
TOTAL		N/S 10 TRICKS											• *Trick total*

TRICK SUMMARY
Tables like this summarize the playing of a hand. Each column shows the cards played on one trick. The card led is at the top of each column. Winning cards are highlighted, in red for N/S and in green for E/W. The number of tricks won by each side is at the bottom. In this case N/S make the ten tricks they bid.

— STACKING TRICKS —

Play will continue from Trick 4 until all 52 cards (13 tricks) have been played. Each side collects the tricks that they win and stacks them in a neat pile on the table, as shown below. The tricks are counted at the end to verify whether or not the declarer has made the tricks she said she would. Tricks should be stacked in such a way that you can tell at a glance how many each side has won.

The trick stack

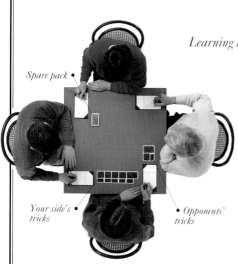

Spare pack

Your side's tricks

Opponents' tricks

SCORING

Learning how to score points and win a rubber

WINNING A GAME

The important thing in bridge scoring is that you score points in two main ways – by bidding and making a contract, or by defeating one bid by your opponents. The other crucial factor is that some contracts are worth much more than others. Is the contract your side bid worth enough to score a **game** (100 points or more)? You need two games to win a **rubber**.

• SLAM CONTRACTS
Bids to make 12 or 13 tricks (eg 6♦, 7♥) are **slam** contracts and attract big bonuses – from 500 to 1,500 points – if made.

• GAME CONTRACTS
To score a **game** you must bid and make nine tricks in NT (3NT), 10 in ♠ or ♥ (4♠ or 4♥), or 11 in ♦ or ♣ (5♦ or 5♣).

• PART-SCORES
Contracts worth less than 100 points are **part-scores**. Part-scores can be added together to make a **game** score.

WHICH CONTRACT?

The trick scores for all 35 contracts are given in this table. Note that the tricks in No Trumps contracts score more than those in trump contracts. 2NT is worth 70 points whereas 2♥ is worth only 60. You can also see that contracts fall into three types: **part-scores**, **games**, and **slams**.

BID	NO TRUMP	♠	♥	♦	♣	TRICKS
7	220	210	210	140	140	13
6	190	180	180	120	120	12
5	160	150	150	100	100	11
4	130	120	120	80	80	10
3	100	90	90	60	60	9
2	70	60	60	40	40	8
1	40	30	30	20	20	7
TRICK SCORE	*First trick 40* *Other tricks 30*	*Each trick 30*	*Each trick 30*	*Each trick 20*	*Each trick 20*	UNDBLD

EXTRA TRICKS
Overtricks – tricks won over those bid – score a bonus, but do not count towards **game**.

TRICK VALUES
For each **overtrick**, your bonus is the value of that trick (bottom line above).

RUBBER BONUSES
You score a bonus of 700, for winning two games to nil, or 500, for two games to one.

Contract	Fails By (Tricks)	1	2	3	4	5
Undoubled	Not Vulnerable	50	100	150	200	250
	Vulnerable	100	200	300	400	500
Doubled	Not Vulnerable	100	300	500	800	1100
	Vulnerable	200	500	800	1100	1400

PENALTY POINT TABLE
If you fail to make a contract, you concede a penalty to your opponents. The more tricks you fall short by, the greater the penalty.

DOUBLING

Any player can **double** a contract bid by one of their opponents if they think that it will fail. The penalty points received are greatly increased if the contract fails (see table above). If your opponents make a contract you have doubled they score twice the amount for the contract and 50 extra points for the "insult".

BONUS OR PENALTY

Play continues in bridge for as long as it takes for one side to score two **games**. The score for each deal is entered once all the tricks are played. The final score is only tallied at the end of the **rubber**. Points fall into two catagories: below-the-line (scores for bidding and making a contract) and above-the-line (penalties and bonuses).
Vulnerability: What you can score in bridge changes when you score the first of the two games you need to win a rubber. Your side is now said to be vulnerable. The penalties for failing to make a contract you bid go up as do the bonuses for making a **slam** (see table left).
Bonuses: These are scored for **overtricks** and winning the **rubber** (see facing page). There are also bonus points for **slams** – 500 or 750 for a small slam (12 tricks), 1,000 or 1,500 for a grand slam (13 tricks).

THE SCORECARD

SCORING
Here is an example of how a typical **rubber** might be scored. Rubbers can last from two up to ten or more hands. At this stage though, all you need is a rough idea of how the scoring works.
First hand: You fail by two tricks to make a contract you bid. Your opponents score 100 penalty points above-the-line.
Second hand: You bid and make a **game** (4♠) with a contract worth 120 points. A line is drawn under this score to mark the winning of a game.
Third hand: You bid and make 3NT, a second game contract (worth 100 points). This means your side has won a **rubber**. This earns you a rubber bonus of 700 points.

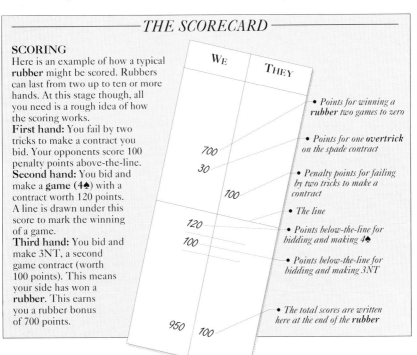

- Points for winning a rubber two games to zero
- Points for one **overtrick** on the spade contract
- Penalty points for failing by two tricks to make a contract
- The line
- Points below-the-line for bidding and making 4♠
- Points below-the-line for bidding and making 3NT
- The total scores are written here at the end of the **rubber**

WE: 700, 30, 120, 100, 950
THEY: 100, 100

THE WEEKEND COURSE

The basic skills you need for success at bridge

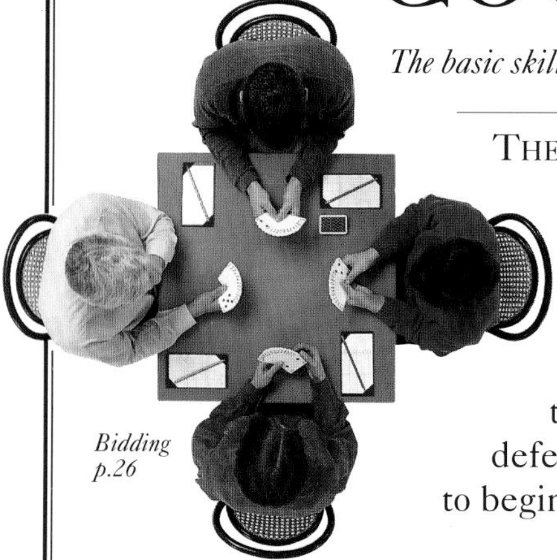

•

THE COURSE COVERS 13 basic skills in two days. Your first day will lead you through valuing and bidding your hand, and winning tricks in trumps and No Trumps. The second day you will be tackling more advanced techniques, competitive bidding, and defence. By the end, you should be ready to begin playing bridge – with confidence.

Bidding p.26

The dummy p.43

High cards p.38

DAY 1		Rating	Page
SKILL 1	Valuing your hand	••	24-25
SKILL 2	Opener's bids	•••	26-29
SKILL 3	Reassessing your hand	••	30-31
SKILL 4	Responding	•••	32-35
SKILL 5	Winning tricks	••	36-41

Low cards p.40

Bridge etiquette p.82

KEY TO SYMBOLS

CARD SYMBOLS
This book frequently uses symbols to represent individual cards and bids. These should not be confused. If a symbol appears like this: ♦3, it represents a card (the three of diamonds). If it appears in reverse: 3♦, it represents a bid ("Three diamonds"). In the notation hands, cards appear as numbers or letters (3 for the three, J for the Jack, and so on). The suit is marked next to the notation. Arrows are used to indicate the direction of play. Where appropriate, a bidding summary table appears beneath the notation hands to indicate the progress of the **auction**.

RATINGS •••••
The rating system in this book indicates the complexity of a skill. One bullet (•) denotes that the skill is comparatively easy. Five bullets (•••••) indicate a more challenging skill that you may not be able to master fully in just one weekend.

PACK OF CARDS
Use a pack of cards to work through all the exercises and examples in this book. Deal out the cards as specified in the exercises, or sort them out into the hands shown by the examples.

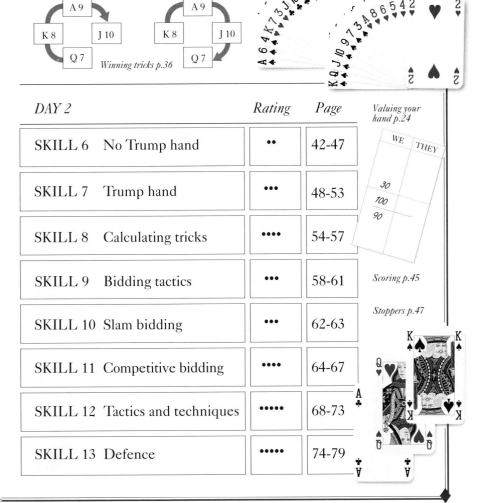

	A 9	
K 8		J 10
	Q 7	

	A 9	
K 8		J 10
	Q 7	

Winning tricks p.36

DAY 2		Rating	Page
SKILL 6	No Trump hand	••	42-47
SKILL 7	Trump hand	•••	48-53
SKILL 8	Calculating tricks	••••	54-57
SKILL 9	Bidding tactics	•••	58-61
SKILL 10	Slam bidding	•••	62-63
SKILL 11	Competitive bidding	••••	64-67
SKILL 12	Tactics and techniques	•••••	68-73
SKILL 13	Defence	•••••	74-79

Valuing your hand p.24

WE	THEY
30	
100	
90	

Scoring p.45

Stoppers p.47

1

VALUING YOUR HAND

Definition: *Assessing the strength and potential of your cards*

WHEN YOU BID AT BRIDGE, your aim is to work out how many tricks you think your side can make. To do that, you clearly need some method of assessing what your hand is worth. Otherwise you won't know how high or low to bid, or whether to bid at all. The way you value your hand at bridge is firstly by applying a simple numerical system known as point-count to your high cards, and secondly by assessing the shape of your hand.

OBJECTIVE: To learn to value your hand for bidding. *Rating* ••

POINTS & SHAPE

How to allot points for high cards and measure shape

POINT-COUNT

The point-count system works like this. Each high card in your hand is allotted a numerical value – so many high-card points. Four points are awarded for an Ace, 3 for a King, 2 for a Queen, and 1 for a Jack. With a total of 40 high-card points in a pack, an average hand has 10 points. By adding up the points in your hand, you can see at once whether your hand is above or below average in high-card strength. So it is only logical to use your hand's high-card points total to help you decide whether or not your hand justifies a bid. Later, after your partner has bid, you will also find the point-count system useful in trying to estimate the combined strength of your two hands.

• HIGH-CARD POINTS

The 4-3-2-1 scale slightly undervalues Aces, but is still a useful start in valuing the trick-taking potential of your high cards.

SHAPE

Having counted up your high-card points, you should then look at the shape of your hand – the distribution of its suits – which can also have a big impact on how many tricks you can win. A hand is described as either **balanced** or **unbalanced**, depending on the number of cards of each suit that it contains.

BALANCED AND UNBALANCED

Balanced hands are hands in which there is a similar number of cards in each of the four suits. By contrast, **unbalanced** hands have one or more long suits (more cards in one or more suits than any other). They usually win more tricks if one of those suits is named as trumps.

♠ J 10 7 ♥ 10 8 6 ♣ A 6 4 2 ♦ 8 5 4

A weak balanced hand with just 5 high-card points

♠ A Q J 10 8 ♥ 6 ♣ Q J 9 5 3 ♦ Q 7

An unbalanced hand with two long suits (spades and clubs) and an above average 12 high-card points

BALANCED
This hand has 11 high-card points (♠Q ♥KQ ♦A). You can see from the number of cards in each suit that it is a **balanced** hand, well suited to playing in No Trumps.

TWO-SUITED
This is an unbalanced hand with two long suits (spades and diamonds). It contains a **singleton** (one card) in clubs, and a **doubleton** (two cards) in hearts.

ONE-SUITED
This 18 high-card point hand has two **doubletons** (hearts and clubs) and one long suit. With nearly half the 40 high-card points in the pack, this is a strong hand.

STRONG OR WEAK?

Imagine you have been dealt either hand A or B. You can see that they both have 10 high-card points. Based on what you have learned already, which of the hands would be stronger if spades were trumps? And which would be better suited to a No Trumps contract?

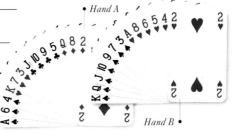

• *Hand A*

Hand B •

SUIT POWER
Hand A is **balanced** and best suited to No Trumps. Hand B will make more tricks if spades are trumps.

MEASURING SHAPE

A common way to measure shape is to count suit lengths. For example, a hand with four cards in spades and hearts, three diamonds, and two clubs, such as hand A (right), is described as 4-4-3-2 in shape. A balanced hand in bridge is one of 4-3-3-3, 4-4-3-2, or 5-3-3-2 shape. You will be dealt such a hand once every two deals.

♠ K Q J 10 ♥ 10 6 5 4 ♦ Q 10 4 ♣ 8 3

A. 4-4-3-2 shape. Is this hand balanced?

♠ K Q J 10 9 7 ♥ 10 6 5 ♦ Q 10 4 ♣ 8

B. 6-3-3-1 shape. Which suit is the strongest?

♠ K Q J 10 9 ♥ 10 6 ♦ Q 10 9 8 4 ♣ 8

C. 5-2-5-1 shape. Which are the long suits?

2 OPENER'S BIDS

Definition: *Making the first positive bid on either side*

HAVING COUNTED THE POINTS in your hand, and looked at its shape, the next step is to learn how to use that information in deciding how to bid. Your first decision, assuming nobody else has made a bid before you, is whether or not to open the bidding. This section describes the different types of opening bid you can make – and how you go about deciding which one to choose. For your bid should give your partner some idea of the strength and shape of your hand. The golden rule is that you want to open the bidding if your hand has 13 high-card points or more – that is, it is three points or more stronger than the average hand. If you have an above-average hand yourself, and nobody else has bid, the odds favour you and your partner being able to make more than half the 13 possible tricks.

OBJECTIVE: To determine the best possible opening bids. *Rating* ●●●

ONE OF A SUIT

If you do decide to open the bidding, on most hands it is best to do so by making a bid at the One Level, as South did on pp.14 and 15. An opening bid of 1♣, 1♦, 1♥, or 1♠ gives your partner this message: "I have a hand with 13 points or more and at least four cards in the suit I have bid." Ideally, to open the bidding, you will have 13 points in high cards alone. However, you can also open the bidding on hands with fewer high-card points if you have a long suit to compensate. For, as well as counting points for the high cards in your hand, you should also add extra points for any long suits you hold. These are called distribution points. The usual scale bridge players use is: 1 point for each five-card suit, 2 for each six-card suit, and 3 for any seven-card suit.

♠ K Q 8 5 4 ♥ 10 ♣ K Q ♦ Q 10 9 8 7

You have 12 high-card points, plus 1 point for each five-card suit. That makes 14 points in all, enough to open on. You will bid 1♠, the higher ranked of the two five-card suits.

♠ Q 9 8 5 4 ♥ K ♣ K Q ♦ J 10 9 3 2

You have 11 high-card points, plus 1 point for each five-card suit. That gives you 13 points, the bare minimum to open. As all your high cards are in the short suits, however, it's safer to pass than open the bidding on this hand.

♠ - ♥ K Q J 9 8 7 ♣ 8 3 ♦ A J 9 4 2

This hand has only 11 high-card points, but count 2 more for the six-card suit and 1 point for a five-card suit. Both the long suits contain good high cards. You should bid 1♥.

♠ A 9 8 6 4 3 ♥ Q J 4 ♣ J 8 5 ♦ K

You have 11 high-card points plus 2 points for the six-card suit. That makes the required 13 points, but the long suit, spades, is poor quality. The singleton ♦K may well not win a trick. You should **pass**.

ONE NO TRUMP

When do you open the bidding with 1NT rather than One of a suit? When you have a strong, balanced hand. In principle, 1NT shows a hand that can win tricks in all four suits. Agree the point-count requirement for 1NT with your partner. If you play a specific bidding system (see pp.90-91), it will be laid down for you. As a beginner at bridge it's best to play a "strong No Trump", which shows a balanced hand of exactly 16, 17, or 18 high-card points.

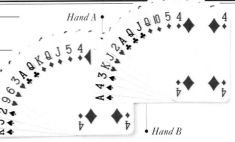

Hand A

Hand B

BALANCED HANDS

Hand A has 16 high-card points and a 5-3-3-2 shape. Although it does not have any heart **honours**, the hand satisfies the requirements for a 1NT bid. Hand B has 17 high-card points and a perfectly **balanced** 4-3-3-3 shape. As it also contains honour cards in all four suits, this hand fulfils all the criteria for a standard 1NT opening bid.

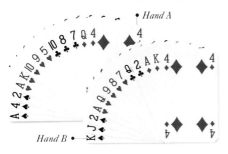

Hand A

Hand B

HAND A

This hand has 13 high-card points plus 1 distribution point for its five-card heart suit. What would you open if you held this hand? The answer is 1♥. This is a good example of a minimum opening bid.

HAND B

Hand B fits the criteria for a **balanced** hand, but it has 19 high-card points (♠KJ ♥AQ ♣Q ♦AK); the maximum strong No Trump opening is 18 points, so you cannot open 1NT. It is close to the maximum strength for opening One of a suit (21 points). You will open with One of the longest suit; that is, 1♥. Your plan is to show the extra strength of the hand by bidding strongly at your next turn.

HAND C

This is a **balanced** hand, but it has only 13 high-card points (♠AK ♥QJ ♦K). You cannot bid 1NT, because to do so you would need 16, 17, or 18 points. Although the hand is balanced, you must bid one of a suit. You hold two four-card suits, diamonds and spades. Bid the lower ranking one first (1♦).

CHOOSING A SUIT

Opening One of a suit is by far the most common opening bid. It covers a wide range of hands – from weak **balanced** hands to much stronger **unbalanced** hands. As your bid suggests a possible trump suit to your partner, you pick the longest suit in your hand as the suit to bid. With two suits of equal length to choose from, as a rule, you will bid the higher ranking (of two five-card suits) and the lower ranking (of two four-card suits).

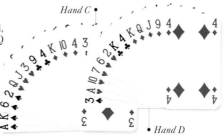

Hand C

Hand D

HAND D

This hand holds 13 high-card points. With a **singleton** (♠3) and a **doubleton** (♣K4), it is an unbalanced hand. Although the diamond suit looks stronger than hearts (with more **honour** cards), you will open 1♥, the higher ranking suit. You will bid diamonds at your next turn to show you have a two-suited hand.

SKILL 2 STRONG TWO BIDS

Some hands are too strong to open with a bid at the One Level. Although it is rare to be dealt a hand with more than 20 high-card points, if you are, you will often need to open with a bid at the Two Level. In most natural bidding systems, 2♣, 2♦, 2♥, and 2♠ are reserved for hands that are so strong you cannot afford to risk your partner passing your bid if he has a weak hand. Such bids tell your partner: "My hand is so strong, we need to go on bidding at least until we have reached a **game** contract".

OPENING 2NT

An opening 2NT also shows a strong hand, but one that is balanced. This 22-point hand (above) is a good example. The normal point-count requirement for 2NT in Standard American is 22 to 24, and in Acol, 20 to 22.

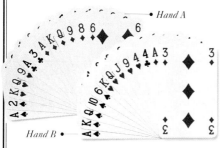

Hand A

Hand B •

POWERFUL HANDS

Holding hand A, with 22 high-card points and a six-card diamond suit, you will open 2♦. Hand B has only 19 high-card points, but eight almost certain tricks, so open 2♠.

TWO-LEVEL NEEDS

How strong does your hand have to be to justify a **game-forcing** bid of two in a suit? This varies from system to system. It also depends on whether your hand's strength derives purely from high cards or from a long and powerful suit instead. But you would normally expect either 22+ points or a strong one- or two-suited hand which you can see will win at least eight or nine tricks on its own.

WEAK THREE BIDS

Bids of 3♣, 3♦, 3♥, and 3♠ are an exception to the rule that an opening bid shows an above-average hand. These bids are **pre-emptive** and weak, designed primarily to obstruct your opponents' bidding. They are typically made on hands with a seven-card suit and 6 to 10 high-card points. Bids of this sort can be very effective. Even if the contract is **doubled** and goes down, the penalty is often fair exchange for the **game** that your opponents could well have made had they bid a contract themselves.

3♥ OPENER

If you make a 3♥ opening bid with this hand, the opposition may find it hard to bid even if they want to. Your long suit ensures you will make some tricks. Similar **pre-emptive bids** can be made at the Four and Five Level.

REBIDDING

On many hands you need more than one bid to show your hand's strength and shape. Unless your partner **passes** your opening bid, you will use your second bid (known as your rebid) to give a more complete picture. If you have a minimum opening bid (13 to 15 points), you will normally rebid at the cheapest level – in No Trumps, the suit bid by your partner, or your own first suit. If you have an above-average hand (16+ points) you may need to **jump** a bidding level.

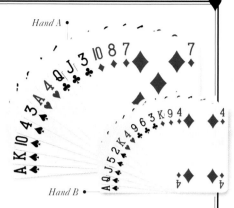

Hand A •

Hand B •

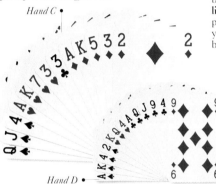

Hand C •

Hand D •

MINIMUM HANDS

Both the hands above are minimum opening bids of 1♠. If your partner has a weak or **limited** hand (eg he bids 1NT or 2♠ – see p.31), you **pass**. If he bids a new suit (eg 2♣), you rebid 2♠, a minimum rebid of the suit you bid first, promising five cards in the suit bid.

STRONG HANDS

Hand C (left) has 17 high-card points. You open 1♦. If partner replies 1♥, you jump raise to 4♥. You have a good trump **fit** and a **game** contract is probable. If he replies 1♠ or 2♣, rebid 2♥ – to show a second suit and stronger-than-minimum opening bid. With hand D (19 high-card points), open 1♣. If partner replies 1♠, raise to 4♠. If partner replies 1♦, 1♥, or 1NT, make a **jump** rebid with 2♠.

KEY PRINCIPLES

Bidding well is an art and not a science. The bidding in this book mainly follows Standard American methods. Bidding systems are designed to give you a framework but they cannot always give you the right answer. Here are some of the key points you have come across so far.
• To open the bidding, you need an above-average hand (13+ points). Bid 1NT with a **balanced** 16-18-point hand, otherwise bid your longest suit first. You are beginning to describe your hand.
• Any bid of a suit guarantees you hold four or more cards in it. To open at the Two Level you need at least five cards in a suit plus a very powerful hand.
• Whenever your side has eight or more cards in a suit, you have a good trump **fit** – and you will normally want to pick that suit as trumps for your final contract.
•Rebidding a suit without support from

When making an opening bid, think about your rebid (your next bid). If you are unable to find a suitable rebid, then your opening bid was probably not the correct one

your partner guarantees five cards in that suit. To bid it three times without support promises six cards.
• Rebidding at the cheapest level is usually how you show a minimum opening hand. With a much stronger hand, you have the option of **jumping** a level when you rebid.
• If your hand is a balanced hand, and if you cannot find a trump fit with your partner, consider bidding No Trumps. You need some high cards or length in all four suits.

3 REASSESSING YOUR HAND

Definition: *Adjusting the value of your hand in relation to your partner's*

WHEN YOU MAKE AN OPENING BID you have no idea what your partner has in his hand. As the bidding progresses, however, you will have more to go on. The two key factors to focus on are how many high-card points your side have between you, and whether or not you have a long suit in common that you can name as trumps in your final bid. For a **part-score** contract you will typically need between 20 and 25 points in your combined hands, for a No Trump or major-suit **game** at least 25 points or more, for a minor-suit **game** 29 to 33 points, for a **small slam** 33 to 37 points, and for a **grand slam**, 37 to 40 points. The better the fit between your two hands, however, the fewer points you may need.

OBJECTIVE: To reassess your hand during the bidding. *Rating* ••

Partner's hand •

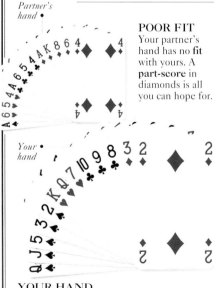

Your • hand

POOR FIT
Your partner's hand has no **fit** with yours. A **part-score** in diamonds is all you can hope for.

YOUR HAND
With only 8 high-card points, not enough for an opening bid, you must wait for your partner to bid to assess your hand's value.

IMPORTANCE OF FIT

Whenever your side has eight or more cards in a suit between you, it will usually pay you to pick that suit as trumps. A good trump fit may mean two or three tricks' difference in what your side can make. Look at the two hands on the left. Your partner has 15 high-card points and you have 8. But you do not have a trump fit, so there is no obvious trump suit to name, and your high cards do not match up well. You will struggle to make eight or nine tricks at most with diamonds as the trump suit. Now imagine that your partner has ♠AK864 ♥A54 ♣4 ♦A986 instead. It is exactly the same 15 points in high cards, but now, thanks to the spade fit, you can make 11 tricks with spades as trumps.

UPGRADING

It makes sense to upgrade your hand when you have found a good trump **fit**. Adding 5 points for a **void**, 3 for a **singleton**, and 1 for a **doubleton** will give you a fairer picture of your hand's worth when your partner bids a suit that you can support (ie, when you have four cards yourself). The short suits are valuable because it means your trumps can be used to trump losers in your partner's hand. The hand on the right improves if your partner opens the bidding in hearts, one of your long suits.

ADDING POINTS
If your partner bids 1♥, upgrade this hand to 12 points – 8 high-card points plus 3 for the **singleton** ♦6 and 1 for the **doubleton** ♠43. The trump **fit** makes it much more valuable.

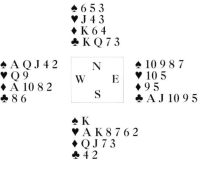

```
            ♠ 6 5 3
            ♥ J 4 3
            ♦ K 6 4
            ♣ K Q 7 3
♠ A Q J 4 2    N       ♠ 10 9 8 7
♥ Q 9      W     E    ♥ 10 5
♦ A 10 8 2     S       ♦ 9 5
♣ 8 6                 ♣ A J 10 9 5
            ♠ K
            ♥ A K 8 7 6 2
            ♦ Q J 7 3
            ♣ 4 2
```

LOWERING VALUE
If West bids spades then South must realize her **singleton** King is exposed and that it therefore loses its potential extra value.

STOPPERS

In trump contracts, you can counter your opponents' strong suits by **ruffing** – playing a trump. But if you intend to bid No Trumps, you need high cards in the other side's long suits – known as **stoppers**. Aces are effective stoppers. Split honour cards, such as KJ5 or Q109, known as **tenace** holdings, are also useful combinations to hold in No Trumps. They are the kind of holdings that ensure you can guard the suit if it is led.

DOWNGRADING

The flip side of this is that you should downgrade your hand if the bidding tells you that you have no trump **fit** – or if it looks as though your high cards may be threatened. On this hand, for example, if West bids spades, South should not count 3 high-card points for the singleton ♠K. It is unlikely to make a trick. The odds must be that West has ♠A. Don't forget that point count is only a guide to help you bid.

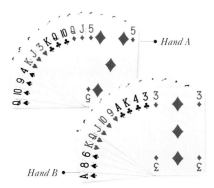

• Hand A

Hand B •

TRUMP OR NO TRUMP?
All four suit holdings in hand A are of the type that play well in No Trump contracts. By contrast, hand B, with its strong hearts, two Aces, and singleton is a good trump hand.

4 RESPONDING

Definition: *The art of replying to an opening bid*

IF YOUR PARTNER HAS MADE AN OPENING BID, you must try to form an accurate idea of the combined strength of your two hands, which will help you judge the level and type of final contract – **part-score**, **game**, or **slam** – you should be considering. Sometimes you will be able to decide the best contract immediately. More often, you will need to start a dialogue with your partner, exchanging information about strength and shape while taking care not to raise the bidding too high on weak or average hands. You can respond with as little as 6 points, and if you have an opening bid yourself (13 points) the chances are that you have enough to make a game contract.

OBJECTIVE: To learn the best response to an opening bid. *Rating* •••

CHOOSE A TARGET

Your partner opens the bidding with One of a suit, and so has at least 13 points in his hand and four cards in that suit. His second bid will tell you more – but start by assuming he has a minimum hand to see where that looks like taking you.

• GAME PROBABLE
If you have 13 or more points, your side has at least 26 (13+13). That should be enough for **game**. You don't want to stop bidding until you get to a game contract.

GAME OR SLAM •
If you have more than 20 points, and your partner opens, your side must have at least 33 points combined – what you typically need to make a **slam** contract.

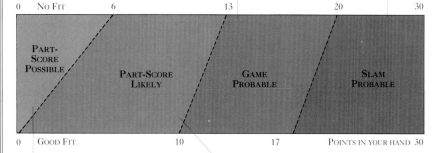

| 0 | No Fit | 6 | | 13 | | 20 | | 30 |

PART-SCORE POSSIBLE / PART-SCORE LIKELY / GAME PROBABLE / SLAM PROBABLE

| 0 | Good Fit | | 10 | | 17 | Points in your hand | 30 |

• PART-SCORE POSSIBLE
With 5 points or less in your hand, a **part-score** is all you can hope for. Your side may not even have the balance of the points. **Pass.**

• PART-SCORE LIKELY
If you hold 6 to 12 points, how high you can go depends on the opener – a **part-score** may be the limit with a **game** possible if he is stronger.

LIMIT BIDS

By making a **limit bid** as your response, you tell your partner: "My hand can be clearly defined within a point or two by this bid." You have no further need to bid again. It is up to your partner to decide what to do. Bids in No Trumps and raises of your partner's suit, are always limit bids. The higher you bid, the more strength you show.

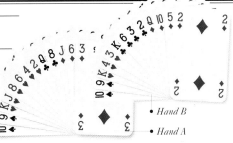

• *Hand B*

• *Hand A*

SAME-LEVEL RESPONSE
On hand A you reply 1♥. On hand B you reply 1NT – a **limit** bid. The 1NT shows 6 to 9 points. Jumps to 2NT or 3NT show stronger **balanced** hands (see pp.90-91).

SINGLE RAISE
Bid 2♠ over partner's 1♠ – this shows 6 to 9 points and four-card trump **support**. Opener can opt to **pass** or bid on.

JUMP RAISE
This hand is too strong for a single raise, so bid 3♥ to show 10 to 12 points – almost enough for **game**.

TRIPLE RAISE
Bid 4♥ over 1♥. A direct **jump** to **game** shows 8 to 12 points, good shape, and excellent trump **support**.

ONE-LEVEL RESPONSE
With the hand above (7 points), you will respond 1♠ to 1♣, 1♦, or 1♥ opening bids. Your partner will rely on you for 6 points if you respond at the One Level. With a weaker hand you **pass**.

TWO-LEVEL RESPONSE
With this 12-point hand (right), respond with 2♣ to bids of 1♦ or 1♥, intending to bid spades or No Trumps later. Two of a suit commits your side to making eight tricks, so you need more points – 10 or more – to bid like this.

SUIT CHANGE BIDS

Your first move on most hands will be to bid in a new suit at the lowest legitimate level, for example 1♠ over 1♥, or 2♣ over 1♠. This requires the opener to bid at least once more. By bidding your long suit first, you offer your partner an alternative trump suit. You may be strong or you may be weak – your next bid can show your partner if you are strong.

SKILL 4
FORCING TO GAME

A **jump** bid in a new suit (for example, 2♠ in response to 1♥, or 3♣ over 1♠), is the way to show a very strong hand if your partner opens. You need at least 16 points to make such a response. The suit bid may be your strongest, or it may be the second suit in a hand with excellent **support** for the opener's suit. After any **game-forcing** bid like this, neither partner will stop bidding until **game** has been reached. A **slam** contract may also be possible to achieve. Wait to hear what else your partner has to say.

RESPONSE TO 1NT: HAND A

Your partner (hand below centre) opens 1NT. With your 5 high-card points **game** is unlikely. Playing with hearts as trumps is going to be better than No Trumps. Remember that the 1NT bid guarantees at least two cards in each suit, so your side must have an eight-card heart **fit**. You bid 2♥, a weak response that the opener must **pass**.

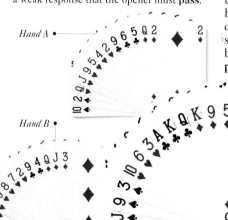

Hand A

RESPONDER'S JUMP

When partner bids 1♣, you see **game** is certain – and **slam** likely. With your 18 points and partner's 13, you have over 30 between you. Bid 2♠. You won't stop below 3NT or 4♠ and could go higher if opener can support spades.

RESPONDING TO 1NT

If partner opens 1NT, you know what he has: a balanced hand, 16 to 18 points, and high cards in at least three suits. By looking at your own hand's point-count and shape, you can mostly tell at once what your side's best contract is. If so, you bid it, expecting the opener to **pass**, as you are now in charge.

Hand B

Opener's hand

Hand C

RESPONSE: HAND B

You have 10 high-card points and a six-card suit. Your side has at least 28 points and a certain eight-card trump suit. **Game** must be a good bet. So you bid 4♥; your partner should then **pass**.

THE OPENER

After bidding 1NT on this hand, the opener will pass if you bid 2♥ or 4♥. The only bid to force him to rebid is Three of a suit. That asks him to bid game in that suit (if he has three-card trump support) or 3NT (if not).

RESPONSE: HAND C

With a 10-point **balanced** hand, you know your side has 26 to 28 points and strong cards in all four suits. Your hand is balanced and you have no long suit to bid, so the right bid now is 3NT. You have the values for **game** – so bid it.

RESPONDER'S REBIDS

PARTNER	YOU
1. 1♠	2♣
2. 2♠	?

• *Your hand*

Once the opener, your partner, has rebid, he will have further defined the strength and shape of his hand. So, by your second bid you can usually see if there is a trump **fit** or if a No Trump contract is more feasible. The options for your rebid include: **passing** (unless your partner has made a strong **forcing** bid); **supporting** a suit bid by the opener; **jumping** to **game** (to show extra strength); rebidding your own suit (to show at least a five-card suit); or bidding a No Trump contract. The two examples on this page show the kind of thinking that might lie behind the decision on a responder's rebid.

BID TO GAME IN SPADES?
You respond to 1♠ with 2♣. This shows 10 or more points and a club suit. Your partner rebids spades. You reason: "I have 13 high-card points. Partner's rebid shows a minimum opener, 13 to 16 points plus five spades. We must have 26 to 29 points. Enough for **game** but not for **slam**. My three spades are good trump **support** if he has five. I bid 4♠."

GAME OR SLAM IN HEARTS?
Round 1. Your hand (left) has 14 high-card points and a good six-card suit. You respond with 1♥ over your partner's bid of 1♦.
Round 2. With his rebid of 3♥, your partner shows four-card heart **support** and a hand strong enough for your side to win nine tricks. You have 10 hearts between you (he raised your suit). Your **singleton** means you will quickly be able to trump diamonds. With ♣A another certain trick, you have 11 tricks in the bag. If you can find one more you could aim for a small **slam** (6♥) contract.

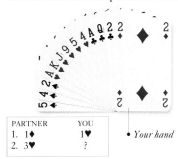

PARTNER	YOU
1. 1♦	1♥
2. 3♥	?

• *Your hand*

STAYMAN CONVENTION

It is best to get basic natural bidding right before exploring more complicated methods. But even using natural bidding, there is always a place for **conventions** – artificial bids that have an agreed meaning different from the obvious one. Stayman is a simple example that you can try out. This convention is a device to ensure you do not miss a 4-4 major trump **fit** after an opening 1NT. In the Stayman convention, a response of 2♣ does not show clubs, but is a conventional bid asking the opener to bid four cards in a major suit. If he cannot do so, he bids 2♦. For example, the bidding might go: A, 1NT ("Strong No Trump"); B, 2♣ ("Do you have a four-card major?"); A, 2♠ ("Yes, a four-card spade suit"); B, 4♠ ("**Game** contract"). The 2♣ bidder only bids 2♣ if he has at least one four-card major suit himself (see p.76).

SAM STAYMAN
The Stayman **convention** is named after Sam Stayman, a well-known American player (above left) who popularized the idea in the 1950s. Hundreds of conventions have been invented over the years. If you do want to explore conventions, the obvious point is that you and your partner must agree which ones you plan to use.

SKILL

DAY 1

5WINNING TRICKS

Definition: *How tricks are won and lost and why it matters*

THE BIDDING AT BRIDGE is only a preliminary to playing the cards. Whether it is your side or your opponents who have bid a contract, the result will turn on how many tricks each side can win. Playing through these simple card exercises will help you get an initial feel for how tricks are won and lost. You will see that tricks can be won in three main ways: with high cards, low cards, and trumps (in trump contracts). You will also discover the importance of being able to deduce who holds the high cards, how to control the lead, and when to lead low in order to win more tricks later.

OBJECTIVE: To learn basic trick-winning techniques. *Rating* ••

FIRST PRINCIPLES

How the cards in your hand can be made to win tricks

WINNING FACTORS

Take the top eight cards in a suit from your pack of cards and deal them out into four hands. Then play them out as tricks, leading from each hand in turn, and noting which side wins most. Three key factors will soon become apparent: the luck of the deal (which side has been dealt the top cards); how the high cards lie in relation to each other; and which hand leads first.

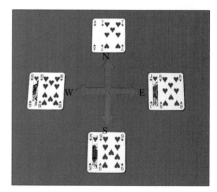

The top eight cards from hearts

SIMPLE TRICK-WINNING

If the cards are dealt like this (above), you will find that the N/S partnership must win two tricks whichever side leads. Their Ace and King are both sure winners. This is the power of high cards. But now see what happens if the Ace and King are dealt to opposing sides. In this case everything depends on where the top cards are to be found in relation to each other around the table.

THE LEAD MATTERS

Look closely at this simple example on the right. Which side should win the most tricks? The answer is: it depends on who leads first. If the first card is played from South, West, or North, you will find that each partnership wins one trick – North with ♥A and East with ♥K. But if it is East who has to lead first, North wins both of the tricks – one with ♥A and one with ♥Q. Variations on this theme occur all the time in the play of the cards. Follow through the examples shown below.

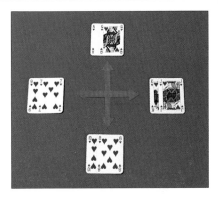

USING THE LEAD

By leading from each position in turn and playing out all eight cards you can see for yourself how the lead can make a difference.

| If South leads the Seven, her side will win only one trick if West (rightly) plays low. | If West has the lead, he cannot win any tricks – whatever he leads, his King falls. | North must lose his Queen to West's King if he leads first – not otherwise, though. | East leads the Queen – now South must play her King to make a trick for her side. |

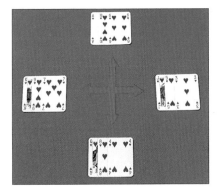

PLAYING THE CARDS

Look at the cards above. Which side should win most tricks? There are many ways the play might go – try it out with your own cards. In almost every case, if each hand plays correctly, the side that leads first cannot avoid letting the other side win two tricks. If you lead a low heart from South's hand, for example, and West plays his lowest heart, N/S cannot win more than one trick whatever card you play from North.

LEADING LOW

With 52 cards in the pack, the number of possible card permutations are more or less endless – so laying down absolute rules about how to play makes very little sense. Some general ideas have stood the test of time well, however. For example, it is usually best to lead **towards** a hand with high cards rather than **away** from it. Many beginners go wrong by leading their high cards at every opportunity. They would do better to save them to beat their opponents' high cards, ensuring that their high cards earn their keep.

SAVE THE ACE

If East leads ♥3, N/S will win two tricks if South plays low, but only one if South plays the Ace or Ten.

HIGH-CARD TRICKS

*Promoting tricks, preserving **entries**, and taking **finesses***

PROMOTING HIGH CARDS

Above are three high-card combinations. In No Trumps, the AKQ will always win three tricks – you simply lead them out in order. With KQJ, you can win two tricks – but only once the other side has played the Ace. You can win one trick with QJ10, but not until you have forced your opponents to play their Ace and King. This technique is known as promoting high cards to winning rank.

CREATING WINNERS

The next step is to look at specific ways in which you can win tricks with high cards. How you play the cards is crucial. In these examples, assume you are South. The cards directly opposite you are in your partner's hand – the dummy. Your aim is to make the maximum number of tricks from the two hands.

HIGH-CARD SPLIT

K 4 3

↑

A Q 2

High cards split between two hands can make as many tricks as the same cards held in one hand. These two hands have the same firepower as the AKQ in just one hand.

DUPLICATION

High cards from a suit in both hands can cancel each other out, however. With six top cards (right), you can win only three tricks if the high cards all fall together.

A Q 10

↕

K J 9

ENTRIES

To win a high-card trick you need two things – the high card itself and the chance to play it. A winning card is no use if you do not have an **entry** (a card that allows you to play your winner) to the hand in which it sits. The importance of entries will come up again and again as you learn more about playing bridge.

♥ A Q ♣ 6 4

♥ 10 ♣ Q J 5 ⬌ ♥ 9 8 7 ♣ 9

♥ K ♣ A K 2

OVERTAKING

You have four winners – two top hearts and two clubs. But unless you play ♥A on your own ♥K, then three will be your limit.

PRESERVING ENTRIES

Why do **entries** matter so much? Look at these three simple card combinations. For example, there are three top cards in spades – but suppose you lead the ♠A first, then a low spade to ♠Q. The ♠K is now a winner, but the lead is in the wrong hand! To keep your entries clear, you must play high cards in the right order – eg ♣4 to the ♣K and then ♣AQJ.

FINESSING

One of the most common high-card manoeuvres in bridge is the **finesse**. This is a way of winning an extra trick by taking advantage of the favourable position of a key card in your opponents' hands. If you hold both the Ace and the Queen in a suit in the same hand, for example, you may be able to win tricks with both of them – so long as the King is held by the player to your right at the table (see below). There are many variants on this idea in the play at bridge. You can often take advantage of where the high cards are positioned.

SIMPLE FINESSE

A Q
↕
7 5

This is the most basic **finesse** position – one that we have already come across. As long as you lead a card from the low-card hand, you can make two tricks if West has the King. If he plays it, you can beat it with the Ace – and if he does not, you can play the Queen and still win the trick. Only if East has the King (a 50-50 chance) will you not succeed in making an extra trick.

LEARNING TO FINESSE

Play through the above examples to see how many tricks you can win.
Spade example: Lead the ♠3 **towards** North's ♠K. You hope that West has the Ace. If he does then your King will win a trick. It does not matter if West plays the Ace on your ♠3 lead or not – you will still win a trick with the King. If East has the Ace, however, this move will fail and he will capture your King with it.
Heart example: Lead ♥J towards ♥AK9. You will win three tricks if West has ♥Q. If East holds the Queen you will win only two tricks.
Club example: Lead ♣2 towards ♣K104 in the other hand. You play ♣10 from the North hand if West plays low – and, as long as West holds the ♣J, you make two tricks for certain.

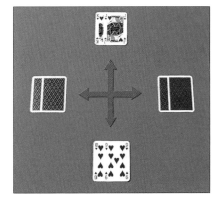

OPPONENTS' POSITION

Suppose you hold the cards dealt to South here. With the ♥KJ in the dummy hand, there is a finesse position available. If West has either ♥A or ♥Q you can win an extra trick by leading **up to** the King and Jack. The snag is you must guess which high card – ♥A or ♥Q – he holds. Bridge would be a lot easier if you could see your opponents' cards!

OPPONENTS' CARDS

It is important to learn to recognize common positions as they arise in play. It will help if you can get into the habit not just of looking at your hand, but of thinking about what cards the other players may hold – or need to hold – if you are to win any tricks.

LEADING LOW

Playing as South you can try a different kind of **finesse** if you have these cards. Lead the Five towards the AJ10, playing the Ten from North if West plays a low card. East will then win this trick with the Queen. When you regain the lead, lead again towards dummy and this time finesse against West's King. This is known as a combination finesse.

LOW-CARD TRICKS

Winning extra tricks can be accomplished by establishing long suits containing low-card winners

LONG SUITS

Why did you count extra points for your long suit when valuing your hand (p.26)? The answer is that low cards in long suits can be just as important as high cards in winning you tricks – if you know where to go and look. Once your opponents have played all the cards they hold in your long suit, any cards remaining in your hand will become winners. Even a Two can win a trick if all the other 12 cards in the suit, from the Ace down to the Three, have been played. These three simple examples will show you how it can be done.

1	2	3	4
S	S	S	S
♣A	♣K	♣Q	♣2
W	W	W	W
♣3	♣7	♣8	♦5
N	N	N	N
♣4	♣5	♣6	♦3
E	E	E	E
♣9	♣10	♣J	♦A

1. LOWEST CARD WINS
Playing as South, lead ♣AKQ. As both opponents follow suit each time, 12 of the suit's 13 cards will have been played. In No Trumps, your ♣2, the 13th card, must win the fourth trick.

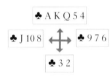

♣AKQ54

♣J108 ✛ ♣976

♣32

2. FIVE TRICKS
As North, you can win five tricks. The ♣5 and ♣4 may both become winners after ♣AKQ are played.

3. SIX TRICKS
By leading ♣AKQ you exhaust your opponents' clubs and turn the ♣762 into winners as well.

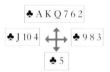

♣AKQ762

♣J104 ✛ ♣983

♣5

SUIT DIVISION

Whenever you have more than half the cards in any suit between your two hands, you will be on the lookout for chances to make an extra trick from the low cards that you hold. The more cards you have in the suit the easier it can be to achieve. The crucial factor that determines how many tricks you can make is whether the rest of the suit – the cards that your opponents hold – are evenly divided between their two hands or not. The more even the division of the opposing cards, the more tricks you can make. The more uneven the distribution, the harder it is.

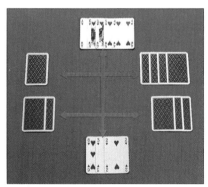

HOW THEY DIVIDE
Play through the example above. You should be able to make five tricks if your opponents' hearts divide 3-2, but not if they split 4-1. The worst possible situation would be if your opponents' hearts split 5-0.

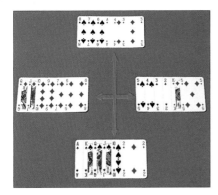

TRUMP POWER
N/S win six tricks if spades are trumps. But if E/W can pick their suit, diamonds, as trumps they will win five tricks with the same cards.

TRUMPS

Trumps are a third weapon in the trick-winning armoury – important both for beating the opponents' high cards and for establishing low cards in your own long suits. The more trump cards one side possesses, the more firepower it has. Consequently, your side's trick-taking potential is increased enormously if you secure the right to choose which suit is trumps. Play through the example, left, first with spades and then with diamonds as trumps, to see what difference choosing trumps can make.

TRUMPS AT WORK

A simple way to put trumps to work is for partners to use the hand with fewer trumps to trump losing cards in their other hand. This will usually create an extra trick. Trumps can also be used to establish low cards in another suit – you keep on trumping low cards until the opponents' cards are exhausted. Deal out the cards as shown, right, and play through the hands as if you were South with spades as the trump suit. The object of the exercise is to make as many tricks as you can by using trumps to create extra tricks out of cards that would otherwise be losers.

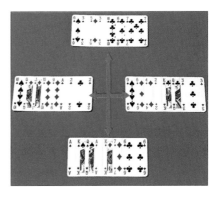

CREATING A WINNER
In the hand above, how many tricks can you make as South, assuming spades are trumps? Answer: it depends on how well you put your trumps to work. If you lead your high cards in order – ♠AKQ, then ♦A and ♦K – you will win five tricks but then you must lose two. If, however, after playing one spade only, you lead ♦A, ♦K, and then ♦7, you can trump this card with ♠8 in North's hand, and one of your two losers has magically disappeared.

CREATING A SIDE SUIT
Deal out the cards as shown, left. Can you make all seven of the tricks this time? The answer is yes. Lead ♠K, from your hand, and then play ♦A, ♦K, and ♦2 from the North hand. Trump the ♦2 with your ♠3 and now – as if by magic – you will have two winning diamonds in the North hand (your opponents have none left). All you need to do is lead your last spade **towards** the ♠A and the diamonds will win you the last two tricks.

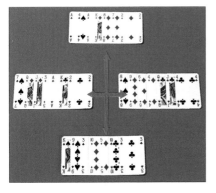

6 NO TRUMP HAND

Definition: *Playing a No Trump contract as declarer*

FOR MANY PEOPLE, playing the hand as declarer is the best part of bridge. You have bid your contract. Now it is up to you to make it. Playing both your hand and the dummy, you have the primary responsibility for a contract's success. In this section we will watch a complete No Trump hand being played from the declarer's point of view. You will see that the key to playing a hand as declarer lies in taking time to think ahead once the dummy is laid down.

OBJECTIVE: To understand the principles of declarer play. *Rating* ••

PLAYING NO TRUMPS

Planning the play starts with the first trick

THE OBJECTIVES

The first thing to be clear about as declarer is what your objectives are. Playing 3NT, your aim is to win a minimum of nine tricks. While you want to make as many tricks as you can, your main objective is to be as certain as possible of making your contract. **Overtricks** are secondary.

	♠ 8 7 2	*Contract: 3NT*
	♥ A J 2	*Lead: ♠K*
	♦ K 6 3	
	♣ K J 10 6	

♠ K Q J 10 9   N   ♠ 5 4
♥ K 6 5   W   E   ♥ 10 9 8 4
♦ 10 4   S   ♦ Q J 9 8 5
♣ 8 3 2   ♣ 7 5

Dealer: South

♠ A 6 3
♥ Q 7 3
♦ A 7 2
♣ A Q 9 4

SOUTH	WEST	NORTH	EAST
1NT	Pass	3NT	Pass

BIDDING
You are South. You deal and then bid 1NT, showing a strong **balanced** hand of 16, 17, or 18 points. With 12 points, North raises to 3NT, the minimum you need to bid if you want to go to game in No Trumps.

WEST LEADS
West leads ♠K. Your partner lays down his hand as the dummy. As the first player to bid No Trumps in the **auction**, you are the declarer on this hand.

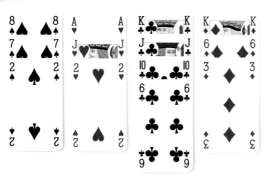

EXTRA TRICK

To find your ninth trick you look through the four suits in your hand and the dummy. The only possible extra winner is in hearts. With ♥AQJ, you can win another trick by forcing out your opponents' ♥K.

WINNERS

When the dummy goes down, pause and work out your plan. In No Trump contracts, you begin by counting your winners. You have eight certain winners between your two hands: ♠A, ♥A, ♦AK, and ♣AKQJ. To make your contract, you must win one more trick. Where will you be able to make this extra trick?

ASSESSING YOUR SUITS

Clubs, spades, and diamonds have high-card winners, but no other trick-winning potential. This leaves hearts, where you may be able to win an extra trick with a **finesse**.

ASSESSING RISKS

As well as developing extra tricks you need to anticipate and guard against what might go wrong. In this No Trump contract the danger is that you are unable to set up your extra winners before E/W manage to establish enough tricks in spades to defeat you. You and your partner have six spades, so you know the defenders must have seven. You can be fairly confident that West has most of them. His ♠K lead suggests that he has led from a long spade **sequence**.

TRICK ONE

You must guard against West establishing his long spade suit. You decide to win the first trick with your ♠A. This gives you the lead.

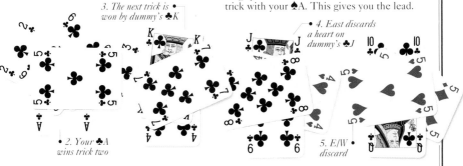

• 3. The next trick is won by dummy's ♣K

• 2. Your ♣A wins trick two

• 4. East discards a heart on dummy's ♣J

5. E/W discard

PLAYING HEARTS

After winning the first five tricks, it is time to tackle the critical suit – hearts. In what order should you play the cards? One way would be to lead a heart from your hand to North's ♥A, and then play ♥Q. Your opponents will beat the Queen with ♥K, promoting dummy's ♥J to a certain future winner. But this will be giving the opponents the lead when they may have four spade winners to play. A **finesse** in hearts is a better option. By leading **towards** dummy's ♥AJ, you can win the extra trick you need at once, if West has ♥K. As the cards lie, you can lead either ♥Q or a low heart first.

TRICK SIX
You lead the ♥Q, intending to play low from the dummy if West also plays low. When West plays ♥K, you win the trick with ♥A. The ♥J in dummy is now established as the next winning trick.

7. ♥J is the seventh trick

COMPLETING PLAY

By now, if you are keeping track, you will know that your 3NT contract is safe. You have won six tricks already, and you have ♥J, ♦A, and ♦K still to play. All you have to do now is to make these remaining winning tricks.

8. ♦A wins trick eight

9. ♦K completes the contract

10. This trick is lost in hearts

11. East's ♦Q wins the trick

12. Your trick-winning resources are exhausted

13. West's ♠Q wins, but too late to defeat the contract

SCORING

Now it is time to enter the score. You made the nine tricks that you bid. 3NT bid and made earns you a trick score of 100 points. As 3NT is a **game** contract, your side is now half way towards winning the **rubber.** Having scored a game you are now **vulnerable** (penalties and bonuses will be greater on the next deal).

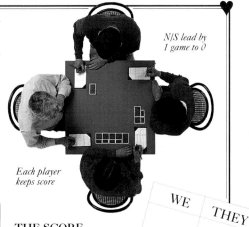

N/S lead by 1 game to 0

Each player keeps score

1	2	3	4	5	6	7	8	9	10	11	12	13
W	S	N	N	S	N	N	S	N	E	E	E	E
♠K	♠A	♣4	♣J	♠10	♥Q	♥J	♦3	♦2	♥2	♦Q	♦J	♠5
N	W	W	E	E	W	E	E	W	E	S	S	S
♣2	♣2	♣3	♥4	♣5	♥K	♥9	♦8	♦10	♥10	♦7	♣3	♣6
E	N	S	S	N	S	S	N	S	S	W	W	W
♠4	♣6	♣K	♣9	♦Q	♥A	♥3	♦A	♣K	♥7	♣10	♣J	♣Q
S	E	W	W	E	W	W	E	W	W	N	N	N
♠A	♣5	♣7	♣8	♥5	♥8	♥6	♦4	♦9	♣9	♦6	♣7	♣8
TOTAL		N/S 9 TRICKS					E/W 4 TRICKS					

REVIEWING THE PLAY
The trick summary (above) allows you to review the hand, trick by trick. Replaying hands is a good way of improving your technique. On pages 46-47 we will go back over the hand and analyse the play further.

THE SCORE
The trick score of 100 points is entered below-the-line on your side of the scorecard. The score is made up of 40 points for the first No Trump trick and 30 for each subsequent one.

GAME SCORED •
As your side has scored a **game**, don't forget to draw a line under the score to remind you of this fact.

BIDDING & SCORING

UNDERBIDDING
Suppose you had bid 2NT (not 3NT) and had made the same nine tricks. Your score would be 70 points below-the-line (for 2NT) and 30 points above (for one **overtrick**). By underbidding you make only a **part-score**, not a **game** contract.

WRONG SUIT
If you had bid 3♣, rather than 3NT, and had made nine tricks, your score below-the-line would only be 60 points – again a **part-score** rather than a **game**. This is because tricks in minor-suit contracts are worth less than in No Trumps.

OVERBIDDING
If instead you had bid 4NT, and had made nine tricks, your contract would have failed by one trick. Your opponents would have scored 50 points above-the-line. This is the penalty for losing a contract by one trick.

DOUBLING
If you were **doubled** in 3NT, and made nine tricks, your score would be: 200 points below-the-line (the trick score of 100 doubled), plus 50 points above. This bonus is given to anyone who makes a doubled contract.

6 CRUCIAL TRICKS

Looking at how you won the hand

WIN OR LOSE

There were two critical moments in this hand – the first and sixth tricks. You decided to win the first trick and to **finesse** at trick six. In fact, had you deliberately lost the first trick, you could have made the contract without relying on the finesse. The following scenario shows how easily the finesse could have led to your defeat.

TRICK ONE
Imagine that East and not West holds the ♥K. West still leads the ♠K, for the same reason as before. The defence want to establish their long suit. You win with ♠A.

TRICK SIX
With everything going as it did before, at trick six you try to take the heart **finesse**, but because East has the ♥K, you lose the trick, and so lose the lead to East. East will now lead a spade.

1	2	3	4	5	6
W	S	S	N	N	S
♠K	♠A	♣4	♦J	♣10	♥Q
N	W	W	E	E	W
♣2	♣2	♣3	♥4	♦5	♥8
E	N	N	S	S	N
♠4	♣6	♣K	♦9	♣Q	♥2
S	E	E	W	W	E
♠A	♣5	♣7	♣8	♥5	♥K

SPADE POSITION

With only six spades and one high card (♠A) in your two hands, the threat from E/W's spades was clear. With seven spades between them, you could not stop them defeating your contract once you lost the lead.

7	8	9	10	11	12	13
E	W	W	W	W	N	N
♠5	♠Q	♠J	♠10	♥6	♦K	♦6
S	N	N	N	N	E	E
♠3	♠8	♦3	♥J	♥A	♣J	♦Q
W	E	E	E	E	S	S
♠9	♠8	♥10	♥9	♦9	♦7	♠A
N	S	S	S	S	W	W
♠7	♠6	♥3	♦2	♥7	♦4	♦10

DEFEAT
The heart **finesse** has lost, and East has led a spade. E/W have enough winning cards to defeat your contract before dummy's ♥A regains the lead.

RELYING ON CHANCE
Now you can see how you could have lost by relying on the 50-50 chance of a **finesse**, which would have failed had East, not West, held the ♥K. So what should you have done?

HOLDING-UP

```
              ♠ 8 7 2
              ♥ A J 2
              ♦ K 6 3
              ♣ K J 10 6
♠ K Q J 10 9      N        ♠ 5 4
♥ 8 6 5                    ♥ K 10 9 4
♦ 10 4       W       E     ♦ Q J 9 8 5
♣ 8 3 2           S        ♣ 7 5
              ♠ A 6 3
              ♥ Q 7 3
              ♦ A 7 2
              ♣ A Q 9 4
```

If you declined to win the first trick (**holding-up** your Ace), West would lead a second spade, which you could then take. This second trick exhausts East's spades. If East has the ♥K, she will still win when you try to **finesse**, but she no longer has a spade to lead **towards** her partner's long suit.

GUARANTEED SUCCESS
By **holding-up** the ♠A for one trick, you are guaranteed to make the contract because, by exhausting East's spades, you have isolated West's winning spades.

LOST ENTRY
Look at the summary box, below. East wins trick seven but she does not have a spade to lead as an entry to West's winners. N/S regain the lead and West's spades never get to win.

1	2	3	4	5	6	7	8	9	10	11	12	13
W	W	S	S	N	N	S	E	N	N	N	S	E
♠K	♠Q	♠A	♠4	♣J	♣10	♥Q	♦Q	♥A	♥J	♦3	♦7	♦J
N	N	W	W	E	E	W	S	E	E	E	W	S
♠2	♠7	♠2	♠3	♦5	♥4	♦6	♦2	♥10	♥9	♦8	♠10	♣6
E	E	N	N	S	S	N	W	S	S	S	N	W
♠4	♠5	♣6	♣K	♣9	♣Q	♥2	♦4	♥3	♥7	♠A	♦6	♠J
S	S	E	E	W	W	E	N	W	W	W	E	N
♠3	♠A	♣5	♣7	♣8	♥5	♥K	♦K	♥8	♦10	♦9	♦9	♠8
TOTAL				N/S 9 Tricks				E/W 4 Tricks				

WINNING BOTH WAYS
How do you know that East has only two spades? You do not. But if East has a third spade, then spades are divided 4-3, which means E/W can only win ♥K and at most three spades (your ♠A wins one) – four tricks in all. So you make your contract anyway.

POINTS TO REMEMBER

STOPPERS
Stoppers stop defenders winning tricks in a long suit. Declarer's tactics will be affected by how many stoppers he has in the opponents' best suit.

PLAN AHEAD
The secret of playing hands well is to think ahead. In a No Trump contract, always count your winners at trick one, that is, before you play a single card.

SUIT COUNT
By adding together your side's cards in a suit, and subtracting them from 13, you can work out how many cards your opponents hold in that particular suit.

TIMING
In most No Trump contracts, you are in a race to set up extra winners – before the other side can set up their long suit. Watch out for what your opponents lead.

SKILL
7
TRUMP HAND

Definition: *Playing a trump contract*

A TRUMP CONTRACT INTRODUCES an extra dimension to the play of the cards. Trumps are powerful ammunition which, if managed carefully, can greatly increase the potential number of tricks your side can win. As declarer in a trump contract, you are less concerned about your opponents establishing winners in their long suits than you are about making the best use of the advantage that winning the **auction** and choosing the trump suit has given you.

OBJECTIVE: To learn how to play a trump contract. *Rating* •••

PLAYING TRUMPS

Planning and playing an effective trump game

FIRST PRIORITY

You are South. You have just bid and made 3NT (see pp.42–47). You have scored **game** and are **vulnerable**. Now you commit your side to making a 4♥ contract – 10 tricks with hearts as trumps. You must work out a plan of campaign. Remember, you can only afford to lose three tricks.

```
                    ♠ 6 5 3        Contract: 4♥
                    ♥ J 4 3        Lead: ♠ J
                    ♦ K 6 4
                    ♣ K Q 7 3
  ♠ J 10 9 7      ┌─────────┐    ♠ A K Q 4 2
  ♥ Q 9           │    N    │    ♥ 10 5
  ♦ J 10 8 7    W │       E │ E  ♦ 9 5
  ♣ 8 6 5         │    S    │    ♣ A J 10 9
                  └─────────┘
                    ♠ 8
 N/S: Vulnerable    ♥ A K 8 7 6 2
 Dealer: West       ♦ A Q 3 2
                    ♣ 4 2
```

WEST	NORTH	EAST	SOUTH
Pass	Pass	1♠	2♥
Pass	3♥	Pass	4♥

THE BIDDING
With a six-card suit and 13 high-card points, you **overcall** East's opening bid. When North supports your hearts, you risk 4♥, a second **game** contract – enough to win the **rubber**.

TAKING STOCK
West leads ♠J. He is leading the top spade in the suit bid by his partner. When your partner lays down the dummy, you should again pause and take stock of the situation.

OUTSIDE TRUMPS

On these two combined hands, you count one loser in clubs (♣A must win), one in spades (your **singleton**), and one possible loser in diamonds (after AKQ have been played).

'LOSING COUNT

As soon as you see the dummy, your first job is to add up your losers. In a trump contract you calculate the losing rather than the winning cards. By assessing the combined holdings, suit by suit, you can see that you may well lose one trick in each suit, which would defeat your contract.

IN TRUMPS

You hold nine hearts, so four are missing. You do not hold the ♥Q. You must hope that the hearts divide evenly and that you can take the ♥Q with your Ace or King.

• TRICK ONE
Your opponents lead their longest suit, and you have no high cards or **stoppers** in spades. You cannot stop West's ♠J winning the first trick, but you can trump spades on the next trick.

• TRICK TWO
Your **singleton** spade proves an advantage, enabling you to trump this spade lead with a low card – ♥2.

TRICK THREE •
You lead out trumps, but your Ace draws only low cards.

DRAWING TRUMPS

The first critical decision, in all trump contracts, is whether to **draw** all your opponents' trumps straight away. It is often right to do so. By eliminating all the trumps, you can prevent your winners in other suits being trumped. But it is not a good idea to exhaust your trumps in dummy too if you need them to trump your own losers.

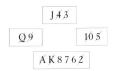

TRUMP BREAK
You hope that the trump suit divides 2-2 between E/W. As you can see above, such a break will neutralize the effect of ♥Q.

TRICK FOUR
Your wishes are answered. The hearts are split 2-2 between E/W, and West's ♥Q does fall under ♥K.

SKILL
7

NON-TRUMP SUITS

Having negotiated the trump suit, the next critical suit to consider is diamonds. With a total of seven diamonds, headed by the AKQ, your fourth diamond can be established as a low-card winner if you are lucky and the missing six cards divide evenly 3-3 between East and West.

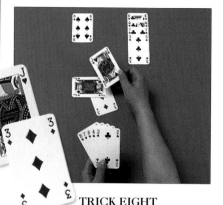

TRICK EIGHT

The 4-2 diamonds split means you hold a potential loser in the suit. How can you get rid of it? By leading the fourth diamond, you can use dummy's last trump, ♥J, to win the trick. Opportunities to trump losers in the dummy are always something to look out for when playing trump contracts.

• 5. Your ♦A wins, leaving ♦K6 in dummy and ♦Q32 in your hand

6. Your next • lead is *towards* ♦K in dummy

• 7. East **discards** a spade, on North's ♦6, telling you that the diamonds have not split 3-3

♦ K 6 4
♦ J 10 8 7	♦ 9 5
♦ A Q 3 2

DIAMOND IMBALANCE

At trick seven, when you see East **discard** instead of playing a diamond, you know that the diamonds are divided 4-2, with West holding four. Remember, East would have had to play a diamond if she had held one.

COMPLETING PLAY

Having got rid of your possible diamond loser, the rest of the play is simple. A trick must be lost to East's ♣A, but as everyone else is out of trumps, yours are all winners.

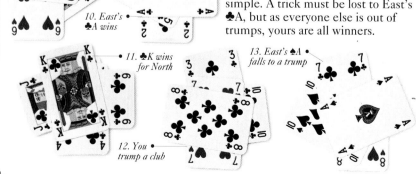

• 9. You trump a spade

10. East's • ♣A wins

• 11. ♣K wins for North

12. You • trump a club

13. East's ♠A • falls to a trump

GAME AND RUBBER

The 100 points below-the-line on the score-card on this page is your score from the No Trump contract (see p.45). On this hand you ended up with 11 tricks – one **overtrick**. As this is a second **game** contract in succession, it means you win the **rubber**. Not all rubbers are over this quickly. There can be many hands of failed contracts or **part-scores**.

BONUSES •
As you have won the **rubber** 2-0, your side gets a rubber bonus of 700 points. The **overtrick** scores a bonus of 30 points.

GAME WON •
You score 120 below-the-line for 4♥ (4x30=120). Your total for the rubber is 950.

			700
			30
			100
			120
			950
WE		THEY

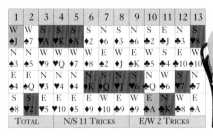

	1	2	3	4	5	6	7	8	9	10	11	12	13
	W	W	S	S	S		S	N	S	N	E	N	S
	♠J	♠7	♥A	♥K	♦A	♦2	♦6	♦3	♠6	♣2	♣J	♣3	♥8
	N	N	W	W	W	W	E	W	E	W	S	E	W
	♠3	♣5	♥9	♥Q	♦7	♦8	♣2	♣J	♣K	♣5	♣4	♠10	♠10
	E	E	N	N		N	S	N	S	N	W	S	N
	♠4	♠Q	♥3	♥4	♦4	♦K	♦Q	♥J	♥6	♣Q	♣6	♥7	♣7
	S		S	E	E	E	E	W	E	W	E	N	E
	♠8	♥2	♥5	♥10	♦5	♦9	♦10	♣9	♣9	♠A	♣K	♣8	♠A
TOTAL				N/S 11 TRICKS				E/W 2 TRICKS					

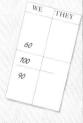

WINNING TRICKS
Reviewing the play shows that you and your partner won three diamond tricks, one club trick, and seven trump tricks. Your diamond loser was "taken care of" by dummy's ♥J.

CHANGING PARTNERS
When a **rubber** has been completed, the players cut for partners. In a social game, unless otherwise agreed, the convention is that players take a new partner for each rubber.

——— EXAMPLES OF SCORING ———

UNDERBIDDING
If you had bid 3♥, but made the same 11 tricks, your side would have scored only 90 points **below-the-line**. You would have a 60-point bonus for the two **overtricks**, but you would have missed **game** and **rubber**.

	60	
	100	
	90	
WE		THEY

VULNERABILITY
If you had been over-ambitious and had bid 6♥, a **slam** call, even if you made 11 tricks you would still have lost a 100-point penalty (one trick down, **vulnerable**, and undoubled), or 200 if E/W had **doubled** your bid, as shown.

		200
	100	
WE		THEY

PENALTY SCORE
Suppose E/W had bid 4♠, to stop you scoring game. Assume that you doubled and E/W made only eight tricks. You would have scored a bonus of 300 points above-the-line, as a penalty against E/W.

	300	
	100	
WE		THEY

BEST OF THREE
If E/W had been able to bid and make **game**, before you made your next game score, then the bonus you would score for winning the **rubber** would be 500 points, because you won the rubber 2-1.

	500	
	30	
	100	
		120
	120	
	750	120
WE		THEY

SKILL 7
TRUMP VARIATIONS
Crucial decisions to make when playing in trumps

QUICK DRAW

The hand you just played highlights the importance of managing trumps correctly. More often than not, it is right to **draw** the opposing trumps at once. A good rule is that you should always do so if you can see an obvious way to make the rest of the tricks you need once you have drawn trumps. If not, then drawing trumps may have to wait while you look for other ways to establish those extra tricks. Do not be deterred from drawing trumps just because you are missing one or more of the top cards in the suit.

TRICK TWO
You may have been happy to trump your opponents' spades with ♥2, but using up your trumps too early can be dangerous.

SLOW DRAW

What would have happened if you had decided to put off **drawing** trumps on this hand? Had you followed this course, you would have taken the risk that one of your opponents would trump one of your winning tricks in another suit. The idea behind drawing trumps is to prevent your opponents scoring their trumps in this way. The only occasions when it pays to allow your opponents to trump your winning cards is when you are confident of winning two extra tricks in return.

PRICE TO PAY
If you lead diamonds before you **draw** trumps, East may be able to trump your ♦Q with a low heart. You may then lose a trick in each suit and fail to make 4♥.

1	2	3	4	5
W	W	S	N	S
♠J	♠7	♦2	♦4	♦Q
N	N	W	E	W
♣3	♣5	♦7	♦9	♦10
E	E	N	S	N
♠4	♣Q	♦K	♦A	♦6
S	S	E	W	E
♠8	♥2	♦5	♦8	♥5

PLAYING OUT TRUMPS
If instead you played out all your trumps as soon as possible (trick summary, right), this too would be a mistake. Even if the opposing trumps fell together under your ♥AK, you would make only nine tricks. Having played your last trump, you would not be able to stop your opponents from playing their winning spades as soon as they regained the lead with ♣A. As a rule, as long as you have trumps left in your hand, you remain in control of play.

1	2	3	4	5	6	7	8	9	10	11	12	13
W	W	S	S	S	N	S	S	S	N	S	E	E
♠J	♠7	♥A	♥K	♥6	♦4	♥8	♥7	♦2	♦6	♣2	♠K	♠A
N	N	W	W	W	E	W	W	W	E	W	S	S
♣3	♣5	♥9	♥Q	♣5	♦5	♣9	♣6	♦8	♦2	♣8	♦3	♣4
E	E	N	N	N	S	N	N	N	S	N	W	W
♠4	♣Q	♥3	♥4	♥J	♦A	♣6	♣3	♦K	♦Q	♣Q	♠10	♦J
S	S	E	E	E	W	E	E	E	W	E	N	N
♠8	♥2	♥5	♥10	♣9	♦7	♣10	♣J	♦9	♦10	♣A	♠7	♣K
TOTAL		N/S 9 Tricks					E/W 4 Tricks					

HANDLING BREAKS

The play on this hand became easy when you realized that E/W's hearts split 2-2. If the split had been uneven, winning would have been more difficult. Here we look at what might have happened with a 3-1 split (right). Planning how to deal with bad trump breaks is vital in trump contracts.

```
            ♠ 6 5 3
            ♥ J 4 3
            ♦ K 6 4
            ♣ K Q 7 3
♠ J 10 9 7   ┌─────────┐   ♠ A K Q 4 2
♥ Q 10 9     │    N    │   ♥ 5
♦ J 10 8 7   │ W     E │   ♦ 9 5
♣ 8 6        │    S    │   ♣ A J 10 9 5
            └─────────┘
            ♠ 8
            ♥ A K 8 7 6 2
            ♦ A Q 3 2
            ♣ 4 2
```

MASTER TRUMP
If East discards at trick four (above right), you will know that West has ♥Q – the crucial card in this hand.

BAD-BREAK HAND
In the hand above, East will **discard** on the second top heart. You then know you have a certain loser in hearts, and you also know that you will lose a spade and a club to ♠A and ♣A. You cannot afford to lose a diamond.

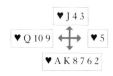

```
            ♥ J 4 3
♥ Q 10 9  ←┼→  ♥ 5
            ♥ A K 8 7 6 2
```

HEARTS DIVIDE
East's **discard** shows you that the heart suit is divided 3-1. The issue now is: do you lead a third heart or not? Playing through the two options (below) shows it is better not to let West win his ♥Q at once.

	1	2	3	4
	W	W	S	S
	♠J	♥7	♥A	♥K
	N	N	W	W
	♠3	♠5	♥9	♥10
	E	E	N	N
	♠4	♠Q	♥3	♥4
	S	S	E	E
	♠8	♥2	♥5	♣5

FIRST OPTION
If you let West win ♥Q at once (left), you will lose the fourth diamond in your hand as dummy's last trump will now have gone.

SECOND OPTION
You must ensure you can trump your ♦3 in dummy (trick eight, right) before West plays ♥Q.

5	6	7	8	9	10	11	12	13
S	W	S	E	S	N	S	N	S
♥6	♠10	♣2	♠A	♣4	♦4	♦2	♦6	♦3
W	N	W	S	W	E	W	E	W
♥Q	♠6	♣8	♥8	♣6	♦5	♦8	♣10	♦J
N	E	N	W	N	S	N	S	N
♥J	♠K	♣Q	♠9	♣K	♦A	♦K	♦Q	♣7
E	S	E	N	E	W	E	W	E
♠2	♥7	♣A	♠3	♣9	♦7	♦9	♦10	♣J

5	6	7	8	9	10	11	12	13
S	S	N	S	N	E	S	N	W
♠A	♦2	♦6	♦3	♣K	♣A	♦4	♦3	♠10
W	W	E	W	E	S	W	E	N
♦7	♦8	♠2	♦J	♥A	♥6	♦8	♣J	♣7
N	N	S	W	N	S	W	S	E
♦4	♦K	♦Q	♥J	♠2	♦9	♣Q	♥7	♠K
E	E	W	E	W	N	E	W	S
♦5	♦9	♦10	♣9	♦6	♣6	♦10	♥Q	♥8

REMEMBERING THE CARDS

Missing trumps

To count trumps first work out how many cards your opponents have, then count down in twos each time both opponents follow suit. If four are missing, two rounds will **draw** them all if they split 2-2.

Remembering which cards have been played is difficult. It helps if you focus on how your opponents' cards divide. If you have a combined eight-card suit, your main concern is whether E/W's cards divide 3-2, 4-1, or 5-0. As long as you count the tricks played in that suit, all you need is to notice when one opponent **discards**. Then you know he holds no more cards in the suit and you can deduce what his partner holds.

SKILL

DAY 2

8 CALCULATING TRICKS

Definition: *How to assess the potential of two hands*

WHEN YOU PLAY A HAND, you must think carefully about how many tricks you need to win to make your contract. As declarer you should get into the habit of scanning your hand and that of dummy, checking each suit for possible winners and losers. Just playing all your high cards first or all your trumps first and leaving the rest to chance will rarely be good enough. You must try to predict how the play of the hand is likely to go – not as hard as it seems.

OBJECTIVE: To analyse how many tricks you can win. *Rating* ••••

ANALYSIS

To practise analysing the combined strength of your hand and your partner's, simply deal out two hands of 13 cards and spend a little time working out how many tricks you think the hands can make. To do this you have to work out where your winners and losers are. Remember that in a trump contract you concentrate on your losers rather than your winners. A certain loser is a low card in one hand matched by a similar low card of the same suit in the other. If you see too many losers, the first thing to do is look for ways of getting rid of them – perhaps by trumping them or **discarding** them on other winners. The more losers you can eliminate in this way the more tricks you can bid and make with your two hands.

SUIT BY SUIT
Matching your hand against partner's you see no losers in spades, clubs, or diamonds. Hearts are the concern.

WHAT CAN YOU MAKE?
With these two hands you can make 12 tricks with spades as trumps. You might think you have three heart losers. But after two heart tricks are played (one won by your ♥A), you will have a **void** in dummy and will be able to trump any other hearts in dummy. In No Trumps, 11 tricks would be your limit.

FOUR LOSERS
You might have four losers – a spade and a club (the two Aces) and two diamonds. This is one too many.

SIDE SUIT

Can you make 4♠ as South with this hand (right)? You have four losers (two hearts, one diamond, and one club). You must use your side-suit (your second long suit), diamonds. After **drawing** trumps, lead the ♦K to force out the Ace. The defenders will play a club or heart next. But you can win this trick with your Ace and **discard** two losers in your hand on the diamond winners you have now promoted in dummy's hand.

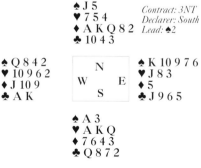

```
        ♠ J 5
        ♥ 7 5 4           Contract: 3NT
        ♦ A K Q 8 2       Declarer: South
        ♣ 10 4 3          Lead: ♠2

♠ Q 8 4 2        N         ♠ K 10 9 7 6
♥ 10 9 6 2    W     E      ♥ J 8 3
♦ J 10 9         S         ♦ 5
♣ A K                      ♣ J 9 6 5

        ♠ A 3
        ♥ A K Q
        ♦ 7 6 4 3
        ♣ Q 8 7 2
```

STRENGTH IN DIAMONDS
Your opponents hold four diamonds. If they split 4-0 you must lose to ♦J. But if they split 3-1 or 2-2 you can make five tricks in the suit to make the 3NT contract.

WEAK SPOTS

You have bid 4♠, undertaking to make 10 tricks. You should be able to make your contract with these hands. The only danger is that opponents lead diamonds, forcing out your Ace. You must decide how to cope with this weak spot before trying to **draw** trumps.

DIAMOND DISCARD
To avoid losing two diamonds, play ♥K, then ♥Q, and **discard** a diamond from the dummy on ♥A. The other side can now take only one diamond once they win with ♠A.

```
        ♠ K 7 6 2         Contract: 4♠
        ♥ A 4 3           Dealer: South
        ♦ Q J 10 8        Lead: ♠J
        ♣ A 3

♠ J 10           N         ♠ 8 5
♥ K 9 5       W     E      ♥ Q J 6 2
♦ 7 6 5          S         ♦ A 9 3 2
♣ K Q 9 5 2                ♣ 10 7 6

        ♠ A Q 9 4 3
        ♥ 10 8 7
        ♦ K 4
        ♣ J 8 4
```

LOSS LIMITATION
Discards on dummy's diamonds will allow you to cut your losers in the other suits.

LOW WINNERS

As South (left), you might think you could make a **game** contract of 5♦, given your strong diamond **fit**. But your opponents have three winners (two clubs and one spade) for sure. Your best game contract is 3NT. You have seven sure winners (three hearts, three diamonds, and one spade). How can you find the other two tricks you need? Use your long suit in diamonds. Once all your opponents' diamonds have been exhausted your low cards will both become winners.

8 SAFETY PLAY

As the declarer, you must often make assumptions about the lie or division of the cards between your opponents' two hands. In this example, your side has bid 4♠. You think to yourself: "We must lose two tricks to ♥A and ♥K. But the contract will only fail if we also lose two trump tricks. With our side holding nine spades, headed by ♠AK, that is unlikely – unless one opponent has all four remaining spades." So your contract is a very good one. You will make it nine times out of ten. Only if one of your opponents has the ♠QJ and two more spades will you go down. Even then you can do something about it – if you spot the danger in good time.

GUARDING
As you have only two losers outside trumps, only a 4-0 trump break can threaten your contract. You can guard against that with a **safety play** in spades.

INSURANCE POLICY
The way to make sure of your contract is to play a low spade from each hand the first time you lead the suit. Recreate the spade suit on this hand and see if you can work out why playing low ensures you need only lose one trump trick at the most.

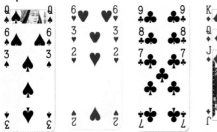

DOUBLE FINESSE
It is unlikely that East has both missing high clubs, but it is possible. Try leading clubs twice from dummy, and **finessing** ♣10 the first time, and ♣Q next. That will make you three club tricks if East does have ♣KJ – your only chance of making the contract. As you play more bridge, you will find more ways to make luck work in your favour, or minimize its effects – but you will never be able to eliminate it altogether.

LOST CAUSES

Sometimes you will find yourself playing a contract that appears to be hopeless. In that case, the best idea is to assume that the cards are favourably placed – if they are not, you lose anyway. Suppose you (South) bid 4♠. It is not a bad contract. But West leads a diamond to his partner's ♦A; a heart is led back and your ♥K loses to West's ♥A. Then your opponents win a second heart and lead diamonds. You have lost three tricks already, and cannot afford to lose any more. Can you think how it might still be possible to make the contract?

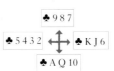

DIAGNOSIS
Your only hope left is to avoid losing a trick in clubs. You must rely on East holding ♣K and ♣J.

CHOOSING TACTICS

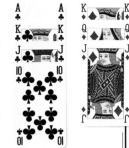

On many hands, you will be faced with choosing between two or more lines of play. Suppose you bid 3NT with these hands (right). You can count seven tricks (♠AK ♥AKQ ♣AK), but you need two more. How would you set up two more tricks? You could try to establish your diamonds, or **finesse** in clubs.

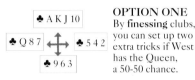

OPTION ONE
By **finessing** clubs, you can set up two extra tricks if West has the Queen, a 50-50 chance.

OPTION TWO
If the diamonds break 3-2, like this, you can establish four winners by forcing out the ♦A.

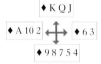

ANALYSIS
Playing 3NT against a spade lead, you have seven tricks. If you cannot find two more quickly you will find that you lose too many spade tricks.

LEAD DIAMONDS
Though it may surprise you, the odds favour leading diamonds. A 3-2 break in the suit is roughly a two-thirds chance, while a **finesse** is only 50-50. For more advanced play you will need to study the odds on suit breaks.

MAXIMUM TRICKS

♠ A K 7 6 2
♥ Q 10
♦ 8 5
♣ A K J 6

♠ 10 8 5 3   ♠ J 9 4
♥ A 8 5 3   ♥ 7
♦ J 10 9   ♦ K Q 7 6 3
♣ 10 2   ♣ Q 9 8 3

```
        N
   W         E
        S
```

♠ Q
♥ K J 9 6 4 2
♦ A 4 2
♣ 7 5 4

NORTH	EAST	SOUTH	WEST
1♠	Pass	2♥	Pass
3♣	Pass	3♥	Pass
4♥	Pass	Pass	Pass

Many beginners might not reach this contract. North opens with 1♠, a bid indicating a minimum of 13 points. You, South, bid 2♥ over the opening bid; this promises at least a five-card heart suit; you hold 10 high-card points. The 3♣ rebid by North shows a second suit, and asks you to

bid again. When you bid 3♥ next it tells your partner that you have six hearts. Even though he only has two hearts, this is enough to justify him raising you to 4♥ with his strong 17-point hand – he knows there are eight hearts between the two hands. Without any high cards in diamonds it would be risky for North to bid 3NT. So he opts for a **game** contract in your longest and strongest combined suit: hearts.

PLAYING THE HAND
This is how the play could develop:
- West will probably lead a diamond, the top card of the only sequence he holds, which you will take with your Ace.
- You will then lead the ♠Q and play low from North. After this you would play a low club to the Ace in North.
- Next you lead your high spades from North, **discarding** a losing diamond on each from your own hand. At this stage you will have won the first five tricks.
- Now all you have to do is to **draw** out the trumps. You will lose one trick to ♥A. After that your trumps are all winners and you will make your contract quite easily.

9 BIDDING TACTICS

Definition: *Bidding in a narrowing field of options*

YOU HAVE ALREADY LEARNED ABOUT opening bids, responding, and rebids (see pp.26-35). This takes you up to the end of the second round of bidding. You will be surprised how often the best contract is already clear at this stage. When there are still decisions left to take, however, your dialogue with your partner must go on. As well as points and trump fit, you also need to keep in mind which final contract is likely to give you the best score.

OBJECTIVE: To judge the best of the remaining possibilities. *Rating* •••

FURTHER BIDDING

What action to take after the first two rounds

NT CONTRACT

When you open 1♦, North responds 1♠, to show you that spades is his longest suit and he has a reasonable hand. Now you will rebid 1NT. This shows a **balanced** hand and 13 to 15 high-card points. At this point North correctly decides to show his four-card heart suit by bidding 2♥. Over this 2♥ you can try 2NT. This tells North you are not strong enough in either of his longer suits for a trump **fit**. But North knows that the partnership is just about strong enough for **game**, with his 12 points plus South's 13 to 15 spread across at least three suits. He decides to bid 3NT. While he knows the contract will be a close run thing, the reward for making game makes it worth a gamble. Stopping in 2NT would only give a **part-score**.

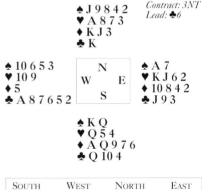

Contract: 3NT
Lead: ♣6

♠ J 9 8 4 2
♥ A 8 7 3
♦ K J 3
♣ K

♠ 10 6 5 3
♥ 10 9
♦ 5
♣ A 8 7 6 5 2

♠ A 7
♥ K J 6 2
♦ 10 8 4 2
♣ J 9 3

♠ K Q
♥ Q 5 4
♦ A Q 9 7 6
♣ Q 10 4

SOUTH	WEST	NORTH	EAST
1♦	Pass	1♠	Pass
1NT	Pass	2♥	Pass
2NT	Pass	3NT	Pass

BANKABLE DIAMONDS

After West's club lead, you have seven tricks (five diamonds, one heart and ♣K) and chances for more in spades and hearts. As the cards lie, your contract will probably come home, making 3NT a worthwhile venture.

TRUMP CONTRACTS

Try to think about your partner's hand and whether your hand will help him. If the bidding shows your side has found an eight-card **fit**, it usually helps to let your partner know at once by bidding or raising his suit. With two possible trump fits, it is often better to play in the one where the cards divide 4-4 rather than 5-3.

Hand A

HAND A

When you open 1♠ and partner bids 3♠, guaranteeing four-card **support**, you know you have enough for **game** and bid 4♠.

Hand D

D AND E
It seems that you have a good **fit** in diamonds with hand D, but count the possible losers.

Hand E

YOUR HAND (HAND E)
If your partner holds hand D or F, you have an excellent diamond **fit**, but do not be too hasty to bid **game** in a minor suit. With hand D as a partner you will lose to ♠AK and ♣A, so a 3NT contract would be better. With hand F you will lose to ♠A and ♣AK. The best contract is 4♥, exploiting the 4-4 heart fit instead.

HAND B WITH C
Your partner, hand B, opens 1♥. You, hand C, respond 1♠. Partner bids 2♥, showing five hearts. Now bid 4♥ – **game** should be on.

Hand B

Hand C

YOUR HAND (HAND C)
The earlier you agree on a trump suit, the better. Do not overlook the fact that three-card trump **support** (if your partner is known to have five cards) or two-card support (if your partner has six cards) is just as valuable as four cards opposite a simple opening bid.

MAJOR OVER MINOR

To make a **game** contract in the minor suits you must bid 5♣ or 5♦ – 11 tricks. You only need nine tricks for a game in No Trumps (3NT) and ten in a major suit contract (4♥ or 4♠) – which is an easier task. So, given the choice, go for the major suit or No Trumps game contract.

Hand F

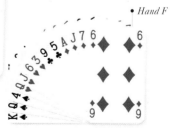

HAND F AND HAND E
If your partner has hand F you want to be playing 4♥, not 5♦. Playing 5♦, missing ♠A and ♣AK, you will fail.

EFFECTIVE BIDDING

Making effective decisions

*North would **pass** 2♥ if his opening bid were a minimum – so South can risk a jump to 4♥*

NORTH	SOUTH
1. 1♥	1♠
2. 2♣	2♥
3. 2♠	4♥

4♥ CONTRACT

You are South, right, trying to find a trump **fit**. Your 2♥ rebid shows three-card **support** for North's 1♥ – with four hearts you would have raised the first time. Similarly, North's bid of 2♠ shows three-card support for your 1♠. Now you know that hearts offer the best trump fit. Why? Because North must have five hearts. His rebid of 2♣ over 1♥ shows at least four clubs, and so five hearts. If he had had four of both suits he would have opened 1♣ (see p.26).

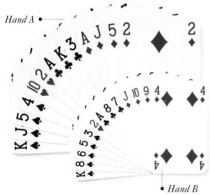

Hand A

Hand B

4♠ CONTRACT

Your partner (hand not shown) opens the bidding with 1♠. How would you best respond with these two hands? *Hand A:* You have 16 high-card points, plus a **doubleton** and spade trump **fit**. **Game** is sure, **slam** possible. **Jump** to 3♦ to show your strength (see p.34). If your partner rebids 3♠, showing a five-card suit, bid 4♠ and wait to see if he can bid on to a slam. *Hand B:* You have 12 points (counting 1 for the five-card suit and 3 for the **singleton**) and a good trump fit. Bid what you think you can make – 4♠.

Auction A

PARTNER	YOU
1. 1♠	3♦
2. 3♠	4♠

Auction B

PARTNER	YOU
1. 1♠	4♠

KEY BIDS

Why do so many of these examples seem to end in bids of 3NT, 4♥, and 4♠? It is the result of the way that the scoring system works. While **slam** hands are exciting when they happen (see pp.62-63), they do not come up all that often. On most hands your real choice lies between bidding a **part-score** and trying to score a

game contract. If you think your side has a good chance of making nine tricks in No Trumps, or ten tricks with hearts or spades as trumps, then 3NT, 4♥, and 4♠ is what you want to end up bidding. There is no point in bidding 4NT, 5♥, or 5♠ unless you are fairly certain a slam is possible – it gets you no extra points.

3♥ CONTRACT

Counting points is a good guide to bidding, but it can lead to penalties if followed slavishly. In points, these two hands (right) are good enough for **game**. But as the bidding reveals, the hands are mismatched. There is no **fit** between North's spades and clubs and South's hearts and diamonds. On badly fitting hands it pays not to be too ambitious – you may well be defeated and end up losing hundreds of points.

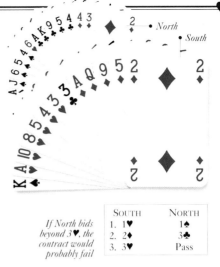

	SOUTH	NORTH
1.	1♥	1♠
2.	2♦	3♣
3.	3♥	Pass

If North bids beyond 3♥, the contract would probably fail

3NT OR 4♠

Either 3NT or 4♠ would be a good contract with these hands (left). In the **auction** South opens the bidding with 1♠ and goes on to show her two-suited hand, asking North for a preference: spades or hearts? With **doubletons** in both suits, North will most likely reply 2NT, since he knows the two hands together are well **balanced**. But 2♠ would also work, leading to a 4♠ **game** contract.

	SOUTH	NORTH
1.	1♠	2♦
2.	2♥	?

North will probably bid 2NT, leading to a successful 3NT contract for N/S

2NT CONTRACT

A vital lesson to learn is to show that you have a limited hand before the bidding goes too high. Not every deal produces **game**. On many hands you must be content with a **part-score**. 2♣ or 2NT would be a good contract with these hands (right). When North comes to bid at his second turn, he bids 2NT – his hand is not quite strong enough (10 points) to risk a game – leaving you to decide how high you want to bid. You have a minimum hand and so you **pass**.

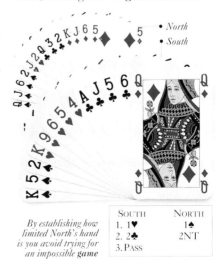

	SOUTH	NORTH
1.	1♥	1♠
2.	2♣	2NT
3.	PASS	

By establishing how limited North's hand is you avoid trying for an impossible game

10 SLAM BIDDING

Definition: *Bidding hands with above-average cards*

THE BASIC PRINCIPLES of bidding strong hands are the same as those for any other bidding sequence. But because they may end in a small **slam**, or a grand slam, they can be more nerve-racking. To make a small slam you must make 12 tricks; to make a grand slam you must make all 13. If your side reaches a **game** contract in the bidding and you have extra strength that your partner does not know about, consider a slam. You must be sure that you have the right number of winners and that you do not have two quick losers.

OBJECTIVE: To learn how to deal with strong hands. *Rating* •••

SLAMS IN A SUIT

In No Trumps you usually need 33 to 34 high-card points between the two hands for a small **slam**, and 37 points or more for a grand slam. In suits, however, slams depend much more on shape and **fit** than on points. As South, can you see how easy it would be for your side to make 6♥? The **singleton** club in your hand means you lose only one club trick. With only 28 of the 40 high-card points you can make 12 tricks.

	♠ A 8	*Contract:* 6♥
	♥ Q 10 4 2	*Lead:* ♣A
	♦ K 10 9 5	
	♣ 8 4 3	

♠ 7 6 2   **N**   ♠ 9 4 3
♥ 9 3   **W**   **E**   ♥ 7 6
♦ 8 6 4   **S**   ♦ Q 7 3 2
♣ A K J 9 5   ♣ Q 10 7 6

♠ K Q J 10 5
♥ A K J 8 5
♦ A J
♣ 2

South's single club means E/W win one trick from ♣AKQJ

	SOUTH	NORTH
1.	1♠	1NT
2.	3♥	4♥
3.	6♥	Pass

JUDGMENT AND CONTROLS

Judging whether you have a good **fit** is crucial when considering a **slam**. If your partner makes a **foreing jump** bid and you have an opening bid yourself, then a slam is always a possibility. Equally, if your partner makes an opening Two bid and you have **support** for his suit or a reasonable hand (8+ points), you will be in slam territory.

You know you will be able to control the play if you hold the Ace and King, or a **void** or **singleton** in a trump contract. Aces and voids are called first-round controls, as they will win the trick the first time the suit is led. **Singletons** and Kings are second-round controls. Controls stop opponents taking too many quick tricks in their long suits.

SLAMS IN NO TRUMPS

In this example (right), both you, as South, and your partner have strong **balanced** hands with 17 high-card points. If you are playing strong No Trumps, the bidding sequence will be very straightforward. When North opens 1NT (a **limit** bid of 16 to 18 points), you can **jump** to 6NT, knowing that your combined point-count is 33, 34, or 35 points (your 17 added to his implied 16 to 18 points). You will be unlucky to fail and in this case can count 12 sure tricks.

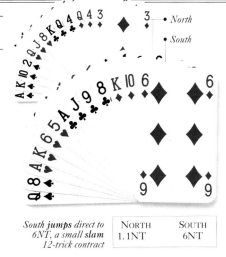

*South **jumps** direct to 6NT, a small slam 12-trick contract*

	NORTH	SOUTH
1.	1NT	6NT

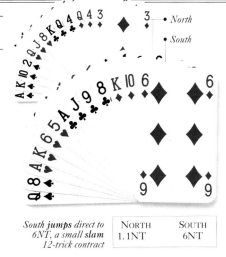

North's 4NT asks: "Have you any Aces?" 5♣ replies "I have no Aces"

	NORTH	SOUTH
1.	1♥	3♥
2.	4NT	5♣
3.	5♥	Pass

NOT OVERBIDDING

North, your partner, opens 1♥. It would be easy, once you have found your heart fit, for North to get carried away with his hand, but by using the Blackwood **convention** (below), a 4NT bid asking you how many Aces you hold, he can discover that you have none and stop the bidding, before it gets too high. To do this he will use a **sign-off** bid: 5♥. Note that you have enough good cards to make 12 tricks – but that is no comfort if your opponents win the first two tricks.

BLACKWOOD CONVENTION

CHECKING ON ACES

Blackwood is probably the most famous **convention** in bridge. The idea is that once a trump suit has been agreed, a bid of 4NT is an artificial bid. It asks partner to show the number of aces in his hand. The replies, also conventional, are: 5♣ shows zero or four Aces, 5♦ one Ace, 5♥ two Aces, and 5♠ three Aces. Each step up shows another Ace. Adding partner's Aces to his own, a Blackwood bidder can see if any Aces are missing. This can be just what he needs to decide if a **slam** is on.

To ask for Kings, bid 5NT: 6♣ shows zero or four Kings, 6♦ one King, 6♥ two Kings, and 6♠ three Kings.

*The 4NT bid was conceived by Easley Blackwood. Many other versions have been developed over the years. Most beginners like to use it. Be warned though that it is only of value on some **slam** hands*

11 COMPETITIVE BIDDING

Definition: *Competitive bidding is an **auction** in which all the players take part.*

BIDDING IS ABOUT assessing risk and reward and making a judgement on the best course of action. This is particularly true in competitive bidding. By bidding against you, your opponents take up valuable bidding space, preventing you from exchanging information with your partner at a safe level. The good news is that by bidding your opponents are also giving you information about their hands. It is possible sometimes to tempt the opposition into bidding too high or frighten them off bidding their contract. Of course, they can always employ the same tactics against you.

OBJECTIVE: Recognizing when to compete. *Rating* ••••

THE DECISION

*Whether it is worth the risk of competing in the **auction***

```
                    ♠ 9 6 3
                    ♥ K 8 4
                    ♦ 8 7 5
                    ♣ K 10 7 3

 ♠ K 4                          ♠ 8 7
 ♥ 7 6 5 3 2      N             ♥ A
 ♦ K J 4 3     W     E          ♦ A Q 10 9 6 2
 ♣ Q 9            S             ♣ J 8 4 2

                    ♠ A Q J 10 5 2
                    ♥ Q J 10 9
                    ♦ —
                    ♣ A 6 5
```

SOUTH	WEST	NORTH	EAST
1♠	Pass	1 NT	2♦
2♥	3♦	3♠	Pass
4♠	5♦	Pass	Pass
		N/S Vulnerable	

SACRIFICE BID
The 5♦ bid is a sacrifice bid. You know that you cannot make 5♦ – but the penalty you concede (even doubled) will cost you less than seeing N/S make their 4♠.

OPPONENTS OPEN

For this example, you are East. You have 11 high-card points and a six-card diamond suit. Your opponents open the bidding. You are reluctant to let them bid alone. Your diamonds could be effective trumps, especially with a **singleton** and a **doubleton** that would soon allow you to **ruff** hearts and spades. You try to see if your partner has a **fit** in your suit by **overcalling**. He bids diamonds at the next level, showing his support but showing no interest in forcing to **game**. You **pass** but N/S find a fit and bid game. West sees that N/S need only this game to win the **rubber** and bids 5♦, to stop them taking the game and the rubber bonus (700 points).

OVERCALLING

If the opponent to your right opens the bidding with one of a suit, you can compete by **overcalling**. You may overcall 1NT, or overcall in a suit at the lowest level (eg 1♥ over 1♦). Or you may overcall in a suit at a higher level (eg 2♥ over 1♦), a **jump** overcall. Or you might make a **pre-emptive** overcall – a double jump (eg 3♥ over 1♦). This shows a weak hand and is designed to disrupt your opponents' bidding. On the right are examples of bids you might make with different hands after 1♥.

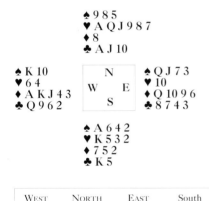

	♠ 9 8 5	
	♥ A Q J 9 8 7	
	♦ 8	
	♣ A J 10	
♠ K 10	**N**	♠ Q J 7 3
♥ 6 4	**W E**	♥ 10
♦ A K J 4 3	**S**	♦ Q 10 9 6
♣ Q 9 6 2		♣ 8 7 4 3
	♠ A 6 4 2	
	♥ K 5 3 2	
	♦ 7 5 2	
	♣ K 5	

WEST	NORTH	EAST	South
1♦	1♥	2♦	3♥
Pass	?		

NO TRUMP OVERCALL

When your partner **overcalls** 1NT he shows 16 to 18 points and a **balanced** hand. It is then up to you to **pass**, move out of No Trumps into a suit bid, or bid to **game** in No Trumps or a suit. Remember, there are only 40 high-card points in the pack – some bidding sequences may make you wonder if there are some extra ones appearing. In these examples (right), your partner has overcalled 1NT after a 1♠ opening bid. How do you bid?

♠ A Q J 10 9 ♥ 4 ♣ 7 6 2 ♦ A 8 5 3

Hand A: **overcall 1♠**. Bids like this show a five-card suit and 10 to 16 high-card points.

♠ A Q 9 ♥ K J 10 8 ♣ A 7 5 ♦ K 9 2

Hand B: **overcall 1NT**. Like an opening 1NT, this promises 16 to 18 points, and **stoppers** in at least three suits.

♠ A K Q J 9 5 ♥ - ♣ J 7 5 2 ♦ A 8 3

Hand C: **jump overcall 2♠**, showing a six-card suit with enough points to open (see p.91).

♠ K J 10 9 8 7 5 ♥ 4 ♣ 5 2 ♦ K Q 7

Hand D: **3♠**, a double **jump** is a **pre-emptive bid**, showing a seven-card suit, but less than 10 high-card points.

SUIT OVERCALLS

Whatever type of **overcall** you make, the final decision on bidding further will be your partner's. All overcalls must show at least a five-card suit, so that your partner has the option of raising the bidding if he has a three-card suit to **fit**. In this **auction** (left) you are South. Your partner overcalls 1♦ with 1♥, indicating at least five hearts. You **jump** to 3♥, telling your partner: "I have heart **support**, it is now up to you whether we bid **game**." Given the strength of his hearts and his **singleton**, he will probably bid 4♥.

♠ 9 4 3 ♥ K 10 8 ♣ K 7 2 ♦ A 7 4 2

Hand A: bid 3NT as you have a **balanced** hand and a combined high-card point-count of at least 26 points.

♠ 9 ♥ J 10 ♣ 8 7 3 2 ♦ K J 8 7 4 2

Hand B: bid 2♦ as you have a weak hand and would prefer to play in diamonds. Your partner must have two diamonds to bid 1NT.

♠ 9 ♥ A Q 10 9 8 ♣ 7 3 2 ♦ A 7 4 2

Hand C: **jump** to 3♥, showing a five-card heart suit. Despite the opponents' bids you have enough points to ask your partner to bid game in 3NT or 4♥.

DOUBLES

*When and why you should **double***

TAKE-OUT DOUBLES

It is not worth your while **doubling** and defeating your opponents' contract at the One Level for the penalty points you would gain. Instead, you double an opening bid to show your partner that you hold 13 points or more, with cards in the unbid suits and usually a shortage in the opposition's suit. This is called a **take-out double**.

Hand A

Hand B

TOO HIGH
You hold hand B (above). You are too strong to overcall 1NT, but you can **double** and bid again after your partner replies.

PERFECT DOUBLE
Imagine that you hold hand A, above. Your opponents open the bidding with 1♥. You hold 13 high-card points, three four-card suits, and a **singleton** heart, the suit bid by the opposition. This is the perfect hand on which to **double**. Your bid asks your partner to bid a suit – and you can **support** whichever of the suits that he chooses.

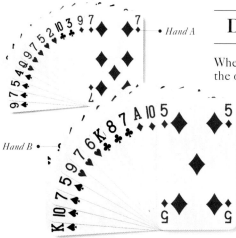

Hand A

Hand B

REPLYING TO A DOUBLE
Imagine you hold either hand A or hand B, above. Your partner has **doubled** a 1♣ or 1♦ opening bid. It is your turn to bid.
Hand A: You bid 1♥, the minimum possible bid, telling your partner you hold a weak hand.
Hand B: With this 10-point hand you **jump** to 2♠. Your partner can bid again or **pass**.

DOUBLES RESPONSE

When you hear your partner **double** the opposition for a **take-out**, you must work out how to respond. The idea at this stage is to show your partner where you strength is. With 0 to 8 points, bid your best suit at the cheapest level. With 9 points make a **jump bid**. You should only bid No Trumps in this situation if you hold extremely good **stoppers** in your opponents' suit. The reason that take-out doubles work so well is that they give your partnership a chance to get into the bidding and find a trump **fit** without the risk of getting too high – and losing a large penalty if you cannot make your contract.

PENALTY DOUBLES

All competitive bidding is a question of how high to bid in the **auction**. If your side has the stronger cards, you weigh what you think you can make from a contract against the rewards from **doubling** your opponents. If you have the weaker cards, you estimate how many points the opponents will score if they reach their best contract, and compare that with what you stand to lose by bidding on and being doubled yourself. The ability to judge accurately how many tricks each side can take will improve with time.

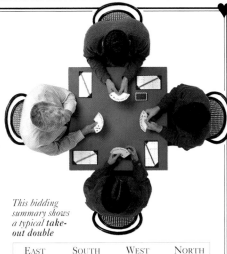

This bidding summary shows a typical take-out double

EAST	SOUTH	WEST	NORTH
1♥	Double	Pass	1♠
2♥	2♠	Pass	Pass

• *Hand A*

Hand B •

LENGTH NOT STRENGTH

Your opponents bid 4♠. If you have hand B, your five trumps will be a nasty shock - a double may work well, better than on hand A.

TO DOUBLE OR NOT

When you **double** your opponents in a high-level contract, you are hoping to score a large penalty if your opponents go down. The biggest penalties come when you have cards they do not expect – such as a lot of their trumps. Remember that the penalties go up if your opponents are **vulnerable**.

BIDDING IN FOURTH SEAT

Whether you get involved in the bidding or not can depend on where you are in the bidding cycle. The more people who have bid before you: the more information you have to work with and the easier it is to judge whether it is safe to intervene. You also need to take the score into account – penalties go up if you are **vulnerable**.

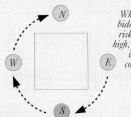

When East opens the bidding, for South the risks of competing are high, as West's strength is unknown. South could well lose a big penalty if West is strong

If West's opening bid is passed around the table, South knows from East's pass that at least one opponent has a weak hand As a result, she will need fewer points to make a bid, because the risks are lower

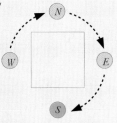

Point requirements for **overcalls** are reduced if the two previous players have passed an opening bid. 1NT now shows only 10 to 12 points, and a **take-out double** may be based on as little as 10 points. Your partner should allow for this when it is his turn to make a bid. Bidding in fourth position is known as protecting.

12 TACTICS & TECHNIQUES

Definition: *Ways and means of putting a plan into action*

THE TACTICS AND TECHNIQUES of good card play are massive subjects. When you first play bridge, you will be happy just to make as many tricks as you can. Later you can start to explore some of the finer points of play. These examples are intended to show you some of the more common manoeuvres that are possible in playing a bridge contract in order to help you to maximize the trick-taking potential of your hand. Play through the examples on these pages with a pack of cards, imagining that you are South.

OBJECTIVE: To understand some well-known techniques. *Rating* •••••

TRICKS OF THE TRADE

Recognizing the need to use strategy and planning to achieve your contract

---

LOSE TO WIN

Sometimes it will make sense for you to lose a trick deliberately. With eight top winners (♠AK ♥AQ ♦AKQ ♣A), you need one extra trick to make this 3NT contract. You identify ♦9 as the potential winner. But if you lead out the ♦AKQ you will fail when the suit divides 4-1. Try it for yourself.

		♠ 8 5 4	*Contract: 3NT*
		♥ 7 6 2	*Lead: ♥4*
		♦ K Q 9 4 2	*Declarer: South*
		♣ J 4	

```
        ♠ 8 5 4
        ♥ 7 6 2
        ♦ K Q 9 4 2
        ♣ J 4
♠ 10 7            N          ♠ Q J 9 3 2
♥ K 10 8 4                   ♥ J 9 5
♦ J 10 8 7    W        E     ♦ 5
♣ Q 9 3           S          ♣ K 10 8 5
        ♠ A K 6
        ♥ A Q 3
        ♦ A 6 3
        ♣ A 7 6 2
```

Key cards

1	2	3	4	5	6	7	8	9	10	11	12	13
W	S	S	W	W	S	N	N	N	E	S	S	S
♥4	♦A	♦3	♥K	♥10	♦6	♦K	♦9	♣J	♦Q	♠A	♠K	♣7
N	W	W	N	N	W	E	E	E	S	W	W	W
♥2	♦7	♦10	♥6	♥7	♦8	♣5	♣8	♣K	♠A	♠9	♥8	♣Q
E	N	N	E	E	N	S	S	S	W	N	N	N
♥J	♦2	♦4	♥9	♥5	♦Q	♣2	♣6	♠6	♠10	♣4	♠5	♠8
S	E	E	S	S	E	W	W	W	N	E	E	E
♥Q	♦5	♠2	♥3	♠A	♠3	♦J	♠7	♦3	♠4	♣10	♠9	♠J
TOTAL	N/S 9 Tricks			E/W 4 Tricks								

RIGHT APPROACH

After leading your ♦A to win trick two, it is better to lose the next one on purpose. When West plays ♦10, you play ♦4 from dummy, instead of ♦Q. **Ducking** a trick like this ensures you still have a card to put the lead back into dummy – a wise precaution when West turns out to have four diamonds.

```
          ♠ K 5            Contract: 3NT
          ♥ A 5 3          Lead: ♠Q
          ♦ A 10 9 8 4     Declarer: South
          ♣ J 5 3
```

```
♠ Q J 10 9 8      N        ♠ 7 6 3
♥ Q J 6       W       E    ♥ 10 9 8 7
♦ 7 5             S        ♦ K 3 2
♣ A 10 8                   ♣ 9 6 4
```

Key cards

```
          ♠ A 4 2
          ♥ K 4 2          West is the
          ♦ Q J 6          danger hand
          ♣ K Q 7 2        with spades
```

TURN TO DIAMONDS

The trick summary shows the right way to play. West holds the danger hand and you must knock out his **entry** (♣A) before he can set up his spades as winners. When East wins with ♦K at trick eight, he has no spades left. If you lead diamonds before clubs your 3NT contract will fail.

AVOIDANCE PLAY

You win the first trick. If you then lead ♣J, East can win with ♣A and lead spades **through** your ♠AQ, setting up West's spades. You must get the lead into dummy and play ♣8 first. If East plays ♣A, it sets up three club tricks as you can keep your ♣KQJ by playing ♣3. If East plays a low club, you can win the trick with ♣J and lead hearts. E/W cannot lead spades up to your ♠AQ without giving you an extra spade winner.

NO ENTRY

For your 3NT contract, you hold five top winners, and need four more. By looking at the dummy and your hand, you can see that there are extra winners in diamonds or clubs. But you must take care to lead the right suit first, otherwise you risk losing three spades, ♣A, and ♦K.

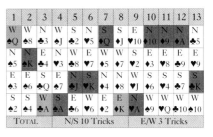

1	2	3	4	5	6	7	8	9	10	11	12	13
W	W	N	W	S	N	S	S	E	N	N	N	N
♠Q	♠8	♠3	♠J	♣2	♥5	♦Q	♦J	♥10	♦10	♦9	♦A	♣5
N		E	N	W	E	W	S	E	E	E	E	N
♠5	♣K	♣4	♥3	♣8	♥7	♦5	♦7	♥2	♦3	♥8	♣9	♥9
E	E	S	E	N	S	N	N	W	S	S	S	
♠3	♣6	♣Q	♣7	♦K	♥K	♦4	♦8	♥J	♦6	♥4	♥7	
S	S	W	S	E	W	E	E	N	W	W	W	
♠2	♠4	♣A	♣A	♣6	♥6	♦2	♦K	♥A	♣9	♥Q	♣10	♠10
TOTAL		N/S 10 Tricks				E/W 3 Tricks						

```
          ♠ 3 2            Contract: 3NT
          ♥ J 5 2          Lead: ♠8
          ♦ A Q J 3        Declarer: South¬
          ♣ K Q 9 8
```

```
♠ K J 9 8 7       N        ♠ 6 5 4
♥ A 7 4       W       E    ♥ 10 9 8 6
♦ 9 8 6           S        ♦ 7 5
♣ 7 6                      ♣ A 10 5 2
```

```
          ♠ A Q 10         Key card
          ♥ K Q 3
          ♦ K 10 4 2
          ♣ J 4 3
```

LEAD THROUGH EAST

As declarer, leading clubs **through** East's hand from North is known as an avoidance play in clubs.

CONTROLLING THE LEAD

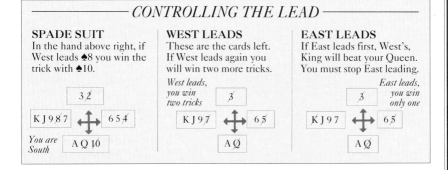

SPADE SUIT
In the hand above right, if West leads ♠8 you win the trick with ♠10.

```
        3 2
K J 9 8 7 <+> 6 5 4
        A Q 10
You are
South
```

WEST LEADS
These are the cards left. If West leads again you will win two more tricks.

```
West leads,
you win        3
two tricks  K J 9 7 <+> 6 5
               A Q
```

EAST LEADS
If East leads first, West's King will beat your Queen. You must stop East leading.

```
                 East leads,
       3         you win
  K J 9 7 <+> 6 5  only one
       A Q
```

12 KEEPING TRUMPS

```
             ♠ 8 3 2        Contract: 3♠
             ♥ 8 7          Lead: ♥A
             ♦ K Q 9 5      Declarer: South
             ♣ A 8 4 3
```

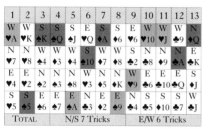

```
♠ 4                    N           ♠ A 9 7 6
♥ A K J 10 9 3     W       E       ♥ Q 6 4 2
♦ 8 7 4 3                          ♦ 2
♣ J 9                  S           ♣ K Q 10 6
```

```
             ♠ K Q J 10 5
             ♥ 5
             ♦ A J 10 6
             ♣ 7 5 2   Key cards
```

In this example, West leads hearts against your 3♠ contract. If you trump and lead spades at trick three, East will **hold-up** ♠A until trick five and then lead hearts, forcing you to trump again. Now only East has a trump left and the contract fails.

1	2	3	4	5	6	7	8	9	10	11	12	13
W	W	S	S	S	E	S	S	E	W	W	W	N
♥A	♥K	♠K	♠Q	♠J	♥Q	♠A	♦6	♥6	♥10	♥J	♣9	♦Q
N	N	W	W	W	S	W	W	S	N	N	N	E
♥7	♥8	♠4	♦4	♦10	♦7	♦8	♠2	♠8	♦9	♠A	♣K	
E	E	N	N	N	W	N	N	W	E	E	E	S
♥4	♥2	♠2	♠3	♠8	♥3	♠5	♦K	♥9	♣6	♣10	♣Q	♦J
S	S	E	E	E	N	E	E	N	S	S	S	W
♥5	♠5	♠6	♠7	♠A	♣3	♦2	♣9	♠4	♠5	♦10	♣7	♣J
TOTAL		N/S 7 Tricks				E/W 6 Tricks						

WINNING PLAY
The trick summary (left) shows how E/W defeated your contract by exhausting your trumps. You should instead **discard** a losing club in trick two, preserving your trumps, and trump any further heart lead in the dummy. Now E/W will not be able to defeat the contract.

```
             ♠ 5 3 2        Contract: 6♥
             ♥ K 9 6        Lead: ♠4
             ♦ A 9 5 4 2    Declarer: South
             ♣ Q 6
```

```
♠ Q 10 9 4             N           ♠ J 8 7
♥ 8                W       E       ♥ 7 3 2
♦ Q 10                             ♦ K J 8 7
♣ J 10 5 4 3 2         S           ♣ 9 8 7
```

```
             ♠ A K 6
             ♥ A Q J 10 5 4
             ♦ 6 3
             ♣ A K
```

ENTRY PROBLEM
After trick one, you must lead diamonds before **drawing** trumps, so as not to exhaust your **entries** to the dummy.

DISCARDED LOSER

In this hand, West leads a low spade against your 6♥ contract. You have two potential losers, a diamond and a spade. To make your contract, you must use your trumps to set up a winning diamond (trick nine), so that you can **discard** your losing spade.

1	2	3	4	5	6	7	8	9	10	11	12	13
W	S	W	S	N	S	N	S	N	N	S	S	S
♠4	♦3	♥8	♦6	♦4	♥4	♦5	♥5	♦9	♦6	♠A	♥A	♠K
N	W	N	E	W	E	W	E	E	W	W	W	W
♠2	♦10	♥6	♦Q	♦J	♣3	♦K	♣9	♣7	♣8	♣J	♠10	♦Q
E	N	E	S	N	S	N	S	S	N	N	N	N
♠J	♦2	♥2	♦A	♥J	♥9	♥Q	♥K	♣6	♣K	♣Q	♠3	♠5
S	E	S	E	W	E	W	E	W	W	E	E	E
♠A	♦7	♥10	♦8	♣2	♥3	♣4	♥7	♣5	♦10	♣9	♦7	♠8
TOTAL		N/S 12 Tricks				E/W 1 Trick						

TRUMPS AS ENTRIES
By trumping diamonds in your hand and using trumps as **entries** to the dummy, you can set up North's ♦9 as the extra trick you need. The key moment comes at the second trick when you lead ♦3 towards the dummy. Play low on this trick. Now, by playing the ♦A (at trick four), and trumping two more diamonds from dummy's hand with your high hearts, you will bring home your **slam** contract.

CROSS-RUFFING

Your contract is 4♠. Do you **draw trumps**? No. That will not bring you enough tricks. You must try to make the most of your trumps separately. You aim to trump hearts from your hand in the dummy, and diamonds from the dummy in your hand.

1	2	3	4	5	6	7	8	9	10	11	12	13
W	S	E	S	S	N	S	N	S	N	S	N	E
♥9	♦5	♣3	♠A	♣2	♦2	♥5	♦3	♥6	♦4	♥8	♦Q	♣6
N	W	S	W	W	E	W	E	W	E	W	E	S
♥10	♦6	♣8	♣3	♦10	♦K	♥4	♥3	♦J	♥Q	♣J	♠5	♣6
E	N	W	N	S	N	S	N	S	N	S	N	W
♥J	♦8	♣4	♣5	♠K	♣10	♦9	♠Q	♠J	♠K	♠A	♠4	♣7
S	E	N	E	E	W	E	W	E	W	E	W	N
♥A	♦10	♣2	♣9	♣8	♦7	♥2	♦9	♥7	♦A	♥K	♣Q	♣7
TOTAL				N/S 10 Tricks				E/W 3 Tricks				

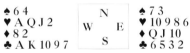

♠ A J 9 2
♥ 10
♦ Q 8 4 3 2
♣ K 7 5

Contract: 4♠
Lead: ♥9
Declarer: South

West:
♠ 7 4
♥ 9 4
♦ A J 9 7 6
♣ Q J 10 3

East:
♠ 6 5 3
♥ K Q J 7 3 2
♦ K 10
♣ 9 8

South:
♠ K Q 10 8
♥ A 8 6 5
♦ 5
♣ A 6 4 2
Key cards

TRUMP POWER

Although E/W lead trumps after winning the first diamond, **cross-ruffing** in this way will bring your side ten tricks (see summary left). Now go back and try to see what will happen if you **draw** E/W's trumps first. You will discover that you have too many losers.

♠ A 10 9
♥ 7 4
♦ A 9 5 4 3
♣ J 8 4

Contract: 4♠
Lead: ♣A
Declarer: South

West:
♠ 6 4
♥ A Q J 2
♦ 8 2
♣ A K 10 9 7

East:
♠ 7 3
♥ 10 9 8 6
♦ Q J 10
♣ 6 5 3 2

South:
Key cards
♠ K Q J 8 5 2
♥ K 5 3
♦ K 7 6
♣ Q

COMBINING LOSERS

After **drawing** trumps, the way out is to play ♣J and **discard** a losing diamond from your hand. This "loser on loser" play gives West the lead. Unlike East, he cannot lead hearts without letting your ♥K win, so you are home.

LOSER ON LOSER

West leads ♣A, and then a trump, against your 4♠ contract. As West, not East has ♥A, you risk losing four tricks – one club, one diamond, and two hearts. Consequently, you must try to set up an extra diamond trick without giving up the lead to East.

1	2	3	4	5	6	7	8	9	10	11	12	13
W	W	N	W	N	W	S	N	S	N	N	N	W
♣A	♣4	♠10	♠J	♠10	♦K	♥7	♦4	♦Q	♦9	♦5	♥4	♥Q
N		E	E	N	W	W	E	W	E	E	E	N
♣4	♣9	♦7	♠3	♠8	♦2	♥8	♦Q	♣7	♥8	♦6	♥9	♥7
E		E	S	N	S	N	S	N	N	S	S	S	E
♣2	♣3	♠5	♦6	♣5	♦3	♦A	♠J	♠A	♥3	♥5	♥K	♥10
S		S	W	S	E	E	W	E	W	W	W	S
♣Q	♣2	♠6	♠K	♣8	♦10	♦J	♥2	♥6	♥J	♣9	♥A	♣K
TOTAL				N/S 10 Tricks				E/W 3 Tricks				

CLAIMING THE CONTRACT

The declarer "makes a claim"

On many hands, declarer may be able to see at a certain point precisely how many of the remaining tricks she can make. If so, she has the option of laying her hand face-up on the table and "making a claim". She might say "the rest are mine". Then the defenders have the right to ask declarer in what order she intends to play the cards.

PLAY IN ACTION

Discovering where your opponents' cards are situated

MISSING CARDS

Building up a picture of the opponents' cards is a key part of learning how to play a hand as declarer. In this example, you are South. You have to make a 7NT contract. The vital clue comes from counting how many cards the opponents have in each of the four suits and where the high cards are. As each trick passes, you will build up a more precise picture of their hands. This will help you to make your contract.

GRAND SLAM

You hold 12 sure tricks – ♠AKQ ♥AKQ ♦AKQJ ♣AK – so you need one more to make 7NT. Your best hope turns out to be an extra trick in the club suit.

1. West leads ♥J, the highest card from a long sequence. The trick is won by your ♥K

*2. East's **discard** on the ♥Q shows she has only one heart*

3. Hunting for more clues, you play high diamonds

4. Both opponents follow suit to the second diamond led. If you can, you want to find out how many cards in the suit each of your opponents holds

5. On your ♦A lead, both opponents follow suit. That means East began with at least three diamonds – as did West

6. SIGNIFICANT DISCARD

You lead ♦Q and East **discards**. Now you can work out that she was dealt three diamonds only – while West had four.

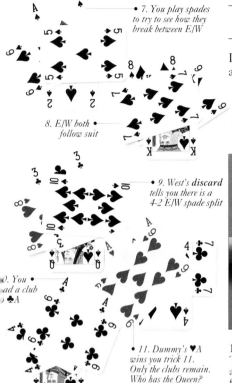

7. You play spades to try to see how they break between E/W

8. E/W both follow suit

9. West's discard tells you there is a 4-2 E/W spade split

10. You lead a club to ♣A

11. Dummy's ♥A wins you trick 11. Only the clubs remain. Who has the Queen?

PLACING SPADES

Leading spades at tricks seven, eight, and nine gives you more clues. Trick nine tells you East was dealt four spades. As she had one heart and three diamonds, her other five cards must all have been clubs.

12. THE CRUNCH
The critical trick. You lead a club from dummy. East follows with a low card. Do you play ♣J or ♣K?

13. You win the last trick

```
              ♠ A 8 3
              ♥ A Q 6 4 3
              ♦ K 8
              ♣ A 9 3
  ♠ 7 6                      ♠ J 10 9 5
  ♥ J 10 9 8 7    N          ♥ 5
  ♦ 10 7 6 5   W   E         ♦ 9 3 2
  ♣ Q 4          S           ♣ 8 7 6 5 2
              ♠ K Q 4 2
Contract: 7NT ♥ K 2
Lead: ♥J     ♦ A Q J 4
              ♣ K J 10
```

FIND THE LADY

The choice is simple. If East has ♣Q left in her hand (having played ♣8), you must play ♣J at trick 12. It will win the trick, leaving ♣K as your 13th winner. But if West has ♣Q you must play ♣K and hope the Queen falls under it, leaving ♣10 as your last winner instead.

1	2	3	4	5	6	7	8	9	10	11	12	13
W	S	N	N	S	S	S	N	S	S	N	N	S
♥J	♥2	♦K	♣8	♠A	♦Q	♠2	♣8	♣Q	♣J	♥A	♣9	♣10
N	W	E	E	W	W	W	E	W	W	E	E	W
♥3	♥7	♦2	♣3	♦7	♣10	♣6	♣9	♥8	♣4	♣7	♣8	♥10
E	N	S	S	N	N	N	S	N	N	S	S	N
♥5	♥Q	♦4	♦J	♥4	♣3	♠A	♣K	♣3	♠A	♣4	♣K	♥6
S	E	W	W	E	E	W	E	E	W	W	S	E
♥K	♣2	♦6	♦5	♦9	♣5	♣5	♣7	♣10	♣6	♥9	♣Q	♣J
TOTAL		N/S 13 TRICKS				E/W 0 TRICKS						

THE FINAL CLUE
You know East had four spades – and she has only played three so far. So her last card cannot be ♣Q. Playing ♣J at trick 12 cannot win – so ♣K must be the right one. It is!

THINKING ABOUT TRICK 12
This is a difficult example – but play through the cards again to see how the **discards** allow you to deduce a complete picture of the opponents' hands.

13 DEFENCE

Definition: *The art of defeating contracts*

DEFENCE IS, SO EVERY EXPERT AGREES, the hardest part
of bridge. There are few extra technical skills required. But
defeating your opponents' contract is harder than playing the hand
because you have much less information to work with than the
declarer. He can see the dummy. You cannot see your partner's hand.
The only way to communicate with each other is through the
bidding and the cards you play. Defending requires a degree of
partnership cooperation and inferential thinking that takes longer
to master than basic card play. Provided you are prepared to make
the effort of keeping up with the play, however, defence can
be every bit as rewarding as playing the hand.

OBJECTIVE: To learn basic defence skills. *Rating* •••••

DETECTIVE WORK

Deducing the best line of defence

DEDUCING OPPONENTS' HANDS
You are West. Your 6-point hand above seems
to have little trick-winning potential. In fact,
you can take heart from the bidding. Both
North and South have shown limited,
balanced hands – and as a result they are
unlikely to have much more than the
minimum 25-26 points you normally need
to make 3NT. Your partner must have 7-10
points and two or three high cards. Your
chances of defeating 3NT are not too bad.

BIDDING SIGNALS

The defenders' task is unambiguous:
to defeat the opponents' contract.
Good defence starts with listening to
the bidding. It can often tell you a lot
about the hands. Does the opponents'
bidding sound strong and confident,
or weak and uncertain? Which player
seems to have the strong hand? Has
declarer bid his trump suit once, or
several times? The answers to these
basic questions will often point you
towards the best line of defence.

SOUTH	WEST	NORTH	EAST
1♦	Pass	1♠	Pass
1NT	Pass	2NT	Pass
3NT	Pass	Pass	Pass

OPENING LEAD

The opening lead is often crucial to the outcome of the hand. Against No Trumps it is normally best to lead your longest suit, hoping to set up extra tricks in it. If your partner has bid a suit, then you should consider leading that suit. Leading from a strong **sequence** (such as KQJ10) is a safe way to start.

Always think before selecting the lead

GETTING INSIDE THEIR HEADS

Try to visualize the cards your partner has – or needs to have – to defeat the opposition's contract. In addition, try to analyse the declarer's play to deduce what he is trying to do and what cards he holds.

ACTIVE AND PASSIVE

There are two ways of defeating a contract. If you attack from the outset, aiming to establish tricks at every opportunity, you are playing an active defence; that is what you are doing when you lead your long suit against No Trumps, for example. Or, you can adopt a passive defence, leaving the declarer to find the tricks he needs on his own. The stronger your opponents' bids, the more aggressively you may have to defend the contract.

WHAT CARD TO LEAD?

There are some well-established rules in bridge about which card to lead in a suit. It is important to know them, since defence, already difficult, would be impossible if partners could not rely on each other leading the same card from a given combination each time. Shown here are some of the more common examples.

The standard lead from a sequence of three or more high cards is the top card – in this example, the King

K Q J 4

↓

Q 8 6 2

↓

With most suits of four or more cards, the normal lead is the fourth highest – in this example, the two

K Q 5 4 2   *With two touching **honours**, lead the fourth highest card*

↓

With three cards headed by an honour you should lead the lowest one...   K 5 3

↓

Q J 9   *...but lead the top card if the suit has two high cards in sequence*

↓

From worthless suits, with no card above a nine, lead the top card   9 6 4

↓

A 5 3   *The normal lead from a suit headed by the Ace is the Ace*

↓

*With a **doubleton**, lead the highest card, with or without an **honour***   9 4

↓

13 DEFENCE PLAY

Using the bids and cards to deduce the best type of play

DEFEATING 3NT

You are West and the contract is 3NT. To beat it you need to make five tricks. From the bid of 1NT you know South has 16, 17, or 18 points. Your most obvious lead is a spade, your longest suit. Lead the ♠J, the top card of a **sequence**. When the dummy goes down, you will find out more about the lie of the cards.

SOUTH	WEST	NORTH	EAST
1 NT	Pass	2♣*	Pass
2♦	Pass	3NT	Pass

*Stayman convention (see p.35)

YOUR HAND
You have been dealt a 6 high-card-point hand. By leading spades you may be able to set up an extra trick if you are lucky.

CARD SIGNALS

When South plays dummy's ♠Q on the ♠J, your partner's card will tell you a lot about who has the other high spades. If your partner has ♠K she will play it now. So when she plays a low spade you know South must hold ♠K.

OPENING LEAD
You can see the 9 high-card points in dummy. As declarer bid 1NT (16 to 18 points) and you have 6 points, you can deduce that your partner has about 8 points. You have a chance.

• *1. Partner plays his lowest spade*

2. Declarer's • ♥K wins

• *3. ♥Q is won by partner's ♥A*

• *4. Partner returns a spade to dummy's Ace*

5. Now dummy • leads a club to South's ♣A

• *6. You discard a diamond*

• *7. South has won seven tricks*

• *8. South's ♣K wins the next trick*

9. Declarer leads ♣J. You win ♣Q. Partner discards

MAKE OR BREAK

You need three more tricks. Holding ♠109 ♦K5, what do you lead? The declarer bid 1NT. If she held ♦A, as well as the other high cards she has shown, she would have had too many points for 1NT. You deduce that your partner has ♦A. So you lead ♦K.

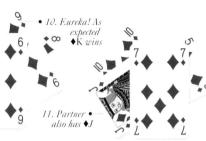

• 10. Eureka! As expected ♦K wins

AFTER TRICK TEN
If South can get the lead back, she has ♠K and another club to win. The only way to stop the contract is to lead ♦K and take as many diamond tricks as you can.

11. Partner • also has ♦J

• 12. East's ♦A is your fifth trick

13. East's ♦4 wins • the last trick too

RECONSTRUCTION
By playing through this example, ticking off the cards, you will see why only the ♦K lead at trick ten beats the contract.

♠ A Q 3
♥ J 10 9 7
♦ Q 10 8
♣ 10 8 5

♠ J 10 9 8   ♠ 7 6 2
♥ 8 6   N   ♥ A 5 4 3
♦ K 5 3   W   E   ♦ A J 9 4
♣ Q 7 6 3   S   ♣ 4 2

♠ K 5 4
♥ K Q 2
♦ 7 6 2
♣ A K J 9

HELP FROM DECLARER
By leading her top cards (♥KQ, ♣AKJ), the declarer made it easier for you to deduce at trick ten that she did not hold the ♦A.

DEFENSIVE MOVES

You are West

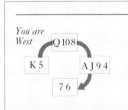   Q 10 8

K 5   A J 9 4

7 6

At trick ten, this was how the diamond suit lay before you led your King **towards** your partner's hand.

Q 10 8

K 5   A J 9 4

7 6

Note how East played his Nine – high cards are often used in this way to signal: "I like your lead".

Q 10 8

K 5   A J 9 4

7 6

After the King, you led your Five and East was able to win the last three tricks with his AJ4.

13 EFFECTIVE DEFENCE
Some common ways to defeat a contract

PRESERVING ENTRIES

Assume you are West defending against 3NT (right). You make a standard opening lead, the fourth highest card in your longest suit, ♠5. South **holds-up** and when you lead a second trick, wins the second trick with ♠K. If South leads diamonds you must not win with ♦K. Let East win the first diamond with ♦A instead. Now East can play her last spade, forcing out ♠A and making your last two spades winners, while you still have ♦K as an **entry**.

```
              ♠ 4 2            Contract: 3NT
              ♥ 5 3 2          Lead: ♠K
              ♦ 8 7 6
              ♣ K Q J 10 9
♠ K Q J 10 8    N        ♠ 9 5 3
♥ 10 8 7     W     E     ♥ 9 6 4
♦ K 10 5        S        ♦ 9 4 3 2
♣ 5 4                    ♣ A 7 6
```

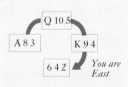

Key cards ♠ A 7 6
♥ A K Q J
♦ A Q J
♣ 8 3 2

KEY CARDS
You attack with ♠K lead. Your partner **holds-up** ♣A for two tricks to exhaust South's clubs.

```
              ♠ 6 3            Contract: 3 NT
              ♥ A K 6          Declarer: South
              ♦ J 9 6 3 2      Lead: ♠5
              ♣ Q 7 3
♠ Q 10 8 5 4    N        ♠ J 9 7
♥ J 10 9 7   W     E     ♥ Q 8 4
♦ K 5           S        ♦ A 4
♣ 5 2                    ♣ J 10 8 6 4
              ♠ A K 2  Key cards
              ♥ 5 3 2
              ♦ Q 10 8 7
              ♣ A K 9
```

KEY CARDS
If you win the trick the first time South leads diamonds, you will not be in a position to defeat the contract.

BLOCKING ENTRIES

As West, you are defending against 3NT (left). Lead the top card from your spade **sequence**. N/S hope to make three extra tricks from clubs. South **ducks** the first two spade tricks until forced to win with ♠A. Now she tries to establish her side's clubs. East ducks twice, on ♣KQ, and then wins with ♣A. If East takes ♣A sooner, 3NT will make. But when ♣A is held up 3NT fails as South has no **entry** to dummy to cash her other clubs.

SIGNALLING MOVES

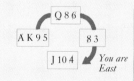

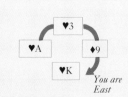

ENCOURAGEMENT
Playing a high card (Nine) can tell partner: "Lead the suit again please".

HIGH-LOW
Play the Eight, then the Three to show partner you have two or four cards.

DISCARDS
A high **discard** (♦9) can tell your partner that you want him to lead the suit.

FORCING TRUMPS

You are West, defending against a 4♥ contract. It is your turn to lead. Your defensive strategy is to exhaust South's trumps, turning your partner's ♥8 into a winner. Your ♠K lead wins the first trick and after that South is forced to trump each time you lead a spade. If South leads trumps East will win with ♥A and lead spades once more. Play the hand through and you will see that E/W must make a total of four tricks however the declarer decides to play the hand.

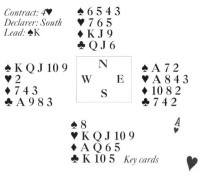

Contract: 4♥
Declarer: South
Lead: ♠K

North: ♠ 6 5 4 3 ♥ 7 6 5 ♦ K J 9 ♣ Q J 6

West: ♠ K Q J 10 9 ♥ 2 ♦ 7 4 3 ♣ A 9 8 3

East: ♠ A 7 2 ♥ A 8 4 3 ♦ 10 8 2 ♣ 7 4 2

South: ♠ 8 ♥ K Q J 10 9 ♦ A Q 6 5 ♣ K 10 5 *Key cards*

LOSING TRUMPS
N/S seem to have only three losers, ♥A, ♣A, and a high spade. But the contract fails as South's trumps run out before East's.

LEADING SINGLETONS

This 4♠ contract (left) looks easy for N/S. As West, you and your partner have only two obvious winners, ♠A and ♥A. It appears that N/S should win 11 tricks. However, if you pick your **singleton** ♥8 as your opening lead, East can win the trick with the Ace and lead ♥2 which you can now trump as you have no hearts left. When East wins ♠A he can then lead another heart back to you, which you will trump. This completes four tricks to defeat the contract.

Contract: 4♠
Declarer: South
Lead: ♥8

North: ♠ 3 2 ♥ K J 4 ♦ A K Q 5 2 ♣ A 8 7

West: ♠ 8 5 4 ♥ 8 ♦ J 10 8 7 ♣ 10 9 6 3 2

East: ♠ A 6 ♥ A 10 9 6 3 2 ♦ 9 6 3 ♣ 5 4

South: ♠ K Q J 10 9 7 ♥ Q 7 5 ♦ 4 ♣ K Q J *Key cards*

KEY CARDS
By leading your **singleton** and trumping hearts you will win four tricks before N/S can do anything about it.

LEADING TRUMPS

You are West defending against a 4♠ contract. If N/S do not **draw** trumps but **cross-ruff** instead, they should make 11 tricks. However, you realize that if you **draw** declarer's and dummy's trumps you can defeat the contract, winning ♥A, ♦A, and two other diamond tricks. Your best possible move is to lead trumps at every opportunity. This removes North's trumps before South, as the declarer, can trump all his losing diamonds in the dummy hand.

North: ♠ K 7 3 ♥ K 9 6 3 2 ♦ 6 ♣ 8 6 5 4

Contract: 4♠
Lead: ♠8

West: ♠ 8 4 ♥ J 10 ♦ A K 4 3 2 ♣ Q J 10 3

East: ♠ 9 6 ♥ A Q 8 7 5 ♦ Q J 5 ♣ 9 7 2

South: ♠ A Q J 10 5 2 ♥ 4 ♦ 10 9 8 7 ♣ A K *Key cards*

KEY CARDS
Play this hand as West, leading trumps whenever you can. You should win two extra diamond tricks once North has no trumps.

AFTER THE WEEKEND

Learning about bridge etiquette, and improving on your techniques and tactics

BY NOW YOU WILL HAVE HAD A CHANCE to get a flavour of what the game of bridge is about, as well as a good grounding in the essential rules of the game. As with all sports and pastimes, there is no better way to complete the learning process than to start playing. Bridge is a very social game, more so than chess or poker, and you can learn a lot from those you choose to play with. How far you want to take your interest in bridge is a matter of personal choice. Millions are content to play it just for fun.

Others thrive on the mental stimulus the game provides, and are keen to go on to investigate its many subtleties and complexities. The paradox is that, while the game is less difficult to learn than many people imagine, the next stage – becoming a good player – requires more effort and application than is often appreciated. Only you can decide how quickly you want to progress, and how much time you wish to devote to playing the game. The one thing of which you can be certain is that bridge's potential to enthral and to entertain is virtually unlimited – after all, there are 635 billion different hands that you can be dealt from a pack of 52 cards. So, even if you spend a lifetime playing the game, you are unlikely to exhaust its rich variety and potential. If you want to read more, there are many books and specialist magazines on the subject. In time, you may want to enter the world of bridge clubs, and consider trying your hand at competitive, or tournament, bridge.

BRIDGE ETIQUETTE

The standards and laws of the game

BRIDGE IS, BY DEFINITION, a social game. Whether in a friendly game, or at a more competitive level, bridge is only a pleasure if it is played in the right spirit. It is important that you are familiar with the laws and proprieties – or etiquette – of the game. At no time should the manner in which you bid or play give you an unfair advantage over your opponents. The laws of bridge are published by the governing body in each country. They include answers to all the common questions that arise during the bidding and play of a hand, such as what to do when a player bids or leads out of turn.

GROUND RULES

It is customary to agree with your partner at the beginning of each **rubber** on the **conventions** and bidding system you intend to play. For example, a typical agreement in a friendly game might be "strong No Trump, Stayman and Blackwood" (see p.27, p.35, and p.63).

Try to avoid bending or marking the cards

PARTNERSHIP

Good technique is not all you need in bridge. It is just as important to have a good relationship with your partner. Mistakes are inevitable, so tact and diplomacy are useful qualities. It is customary to thank your partner when he puts down his cards as dummy (whatever you may privately think of his bidding). As you play more, you may find it rewarding to play with a regular partner.

Remember, bridge is a game to be enjoyed not endured

STAKES
Many players like to play for stakes. Usually a rate is chosen – so much per 100 points. At the end of play, the final amounts of money owing are calculated and settled.

CHANCE
As the luck of the deal does play some part in bridge, some players like to sit in the same seats or play with the same pack for every **rubber**. You must learn to tolerate these quirks.

• TONE OF VOICE
It is improper to make a bid in a particular tone of voice if the effect or the intention is to give useful information to your partner. An example would be **doubling** "in a voice of thunder" to show strength.

• WRONG BID
Bidding out of turn can result in your partner being barred from bidding again.

BIDDING

If you have agreed to play a specific bidding **convention** with your partner, you must let your opponents know. Private understandings are illegal, and bids should be readily intelligible. You are entitled to ask the meaning of an opponent's bid.

HESITATION
It is unethical for partners to hesitate before bidding to try to give you an indication of the strength of his hand. Any player can ask for the bidding to be repeated, at his turn or the end of the **auction**.

FAIR PLAY

Cards should be played in as even a tempo as possible. Do not play out of turn and avoid showing your cards to another player. Once played, cards cannot be retracted.

• STAYING SILENT
Dummy must not tell the declarer what to play, although he can intervene to stop rule-breaking.

• REVOKING
Failure to follow suit when you could do so is known as revoking. Unless the error is discovered immediately, the penalty is to transfer one or two tricks to the other side.

FORBIDDEN LEAD •
If a defender leads out of turn, the declarer can direct, or forbid, the lead of the suit. Cards placed out of turn may become penalty cards – that is, they are left face-up on the table and must be played at the first opportunity.

• CORRECTED LEAD
If the declarer leads a card out of turn, the defenders may accept it if they wish. If the declarer plays from the wrong hand, she must, if possible, lead a card of the same suit from the correct hand.

BETTER BRIDGE

Techniques that will help improve your play

How CAN YOU IMPROVE your bridge? The choice lies
between teaching yourself and learning from experience, and
taking lessons from the experts. According to Rixi Markus, whom
many regard as the greatest woman bridge player of the post-war
age, the quickest way to become good at bridge is to play high-
stakes rubber bridge against players who are better than yourself.
The sheer financial necessity to win will force you to learn fast.
This is true, but most players will no doubt prefer to take a more
measured, less risky approach! You cannot improve your game
without experience, but equally you will not get the most out of
that experience unless you are prepared to spend some time
reviewing and learning from the mistakes that you have made.

TEACHING YOURSELF

Studying bridge hands in newspapers
and books will improve your
analytical powers. Practising
on your own with a pack of
cards will give you a feel for
card play. However, beware of
computer bridge programs as
few are as sophisticated
or as helpful as those
devised for chess.

PRACTISING SOLO
Dealing out sets of four hands
and studying how many tricks
each side can make will help
you to value and bid a hand.

LITERATURE
There is much written
about bridge. Bookshops
and libraries stock many of
the better-known books, and
many papers and magazines
carry regular bridge columns.

REPLAYING
Playing through the hands
again will give you an
insight into how different card
combinations produce tricks. Once
you begin to visualize how the
cards lie, your bridge will improve.

LEARN FROM OTHERS

There is a lot you can learn about bridge from others. Whether discussing a hand that has just been played, or taking lessons from a professional, try to concentrate on why a particular bid has been made or a particular card played. Understanding the logic of good play is more important than trying to memorize rules.

BRIDGE CLUBS
Join a bridge club, or the bridge circle at a club, to play with other enthusiasts.

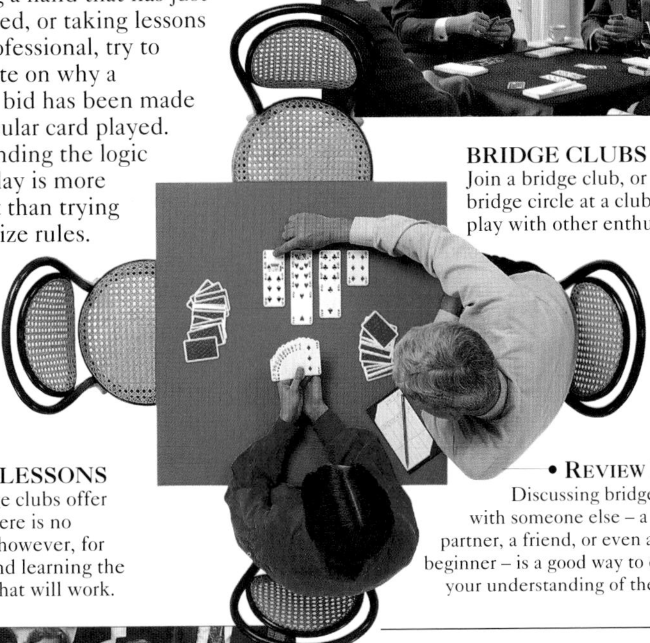

BRIDGE LESSONS
Many bridge clubs offer lessons. There is no substitute, however, for playing – and learning the hard way what will work.

• REVIEW PLAY
Discussing bridge hands with someone else – a regular partner, a friend, or even a fellow beginner – is a good way to deepen your understanding of the game.

EXPERTS AND TOURNAMENTS
Duplicate bridge eliminates the luck of the deal by ensuring that the same hand is dealt again and again to different partnerships. Zia Mahmood seen here (above, far right) is a renowned expert who attracts large crowds.

GLAMOROUS BRIDGE
The film actor Omar Sharif was introduced to bridge during the filming of *Dr Zhivago*. He has since become one of the world's leading bridge players, regularly competing in international duplicate bridge tournaments.

EXPERT EXAMPLE

Bridge is an international sport, having its own world championships and its own Olympics. Although an amateur sport, full-time professional players do exist, particularly in the United States. You do not need to be a world expert to play in many local or national bridge tournaments.

BRIDGE EQUIPMENT

Cards, scorecards, tables, cloths, and added extras

ONCE YOU HAVE LEARNED to play bridge you may decide you want to organize a game or bridge party at your home. A card table is a good investment if you intend to play regularly at home (the table can be easily stored because of its fold-away legs). If you do not have a card table then you can acquire a bridge cloth. This will provide you with a suitable surface from which to pick up the cards. It will also stop them sliding off the table when they are played. Playing cards and scorecards can be found in most department stores and stationery shops. Equipment can also be ordered from specialist bridge suppliers. One of bridge's best features is that it is a game that can be played and enjoyed wherever and whenever you wish.

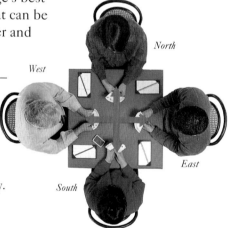

North

West

East

South

PARTNERS

As bridge is a partnership game, the first requirement is a table or playing surface that allows partners to sit opposite each other. They must also be close enough to bid and play easily. Bridge tables are usually square and covered in green baize to make the cards easier to pick up and play.

Bridge tablecloths come in various colours and designs

PLAYING SURFACE
If you do not have a traditional bridge table use a bridge cloth to cover your chosen surface.

A standard-size • bridge table is 69cm (27¹/₂in) high, and 81.5cm (32in) square

SCORECARDS

Scorecards are provided to allow all four players to record the final score of each deal should they wish to do so. A scorecard has two columns and a horizontal line across the middle. The horizontal line is to differentiate between **above-** and **below-the-line** scores. The scorecard is a keen point of interest to all of the players at the end of a **rubber**, especially if there is money riding on the outcome.

Scorecard • columns

Enter your • score in this column

Enter your • opponents' score in this column

WE	THEY
300	
	80

BRIDGE EXTRAS
Specialist outlets supply sets of bridge equipment. These might include two packs of cards, matching scorecards and holders, and bridge pencils. If you wish, you can commission your own personalized set.

SCORE SHEETS
Scorecards are supplied in pads of 25 sheets or more. When one sheet has been filled, it can be torn off and replaced with a new one.

Pencils, scorecards and cards

PLAYING CARDS

It is usual to play bridge with two packs of cards. While one is in play, the other is shuffled and placed on the table, ready for use on the next hand. Alternating packs speeds up the game and also prevents the cards becoming sticky from constant use.

• *Scorecards are placed to the side of each player*

Packs of cards are available in a variety of designs

• *The cards are placed on the table ready for play*

THE HISTORY OF BRIDGE

Bridge has evolved gradually from its beginnings in whist

NOW THAT YOU HAVE LEARNED TO PLAY BRIDGE you might be interested to know a little about where the game began and how it has developed over the years. Bridge is a modern descendent of the game of whist. Bridge inherited from whist the idea of tricks, trumps, and partners, but over the years many other features have been added to it. These have so increased the level of subtlety and skill involved that today the games are hardly comparable.

WHIST TO BRIDGE

In whist four players are dealt 13 cards each and compete in pairs to win the most tricks. Trumps are chosen by turning over the last card dealt. A series of features have been added to create the game of bridge.

THE KEY CHANGES

Early versions of whist introduced a dummy hand and bidding. Auction bridge, which became popular around 1900, was the first complete version of the game that required opposing pairs to compete against each other for the right to nominate the trump suit. Contract bridge, which was devised in the 1920s, and quickly supplanted auction bridge, added a new scoring system that makes accurate bidding the key to success.

CONTRACT BRIDGE

In 1925 Harold S. Vanderbilt devised contract bridge. It is distinguished from earlier forms of bridge by its unique scoring system. Only tricks that the declarer has bid count towards scoring a **game**. This means that it is important not just to outbid the opponents, but to bid the full trick-taking potential of your hand.

Harold S. Vanderbilt

SOCIAL GAME
The immediate predecessor of contract bridge, the game we play today, was auction bridge, a popular social pastime in the early 1900s.

FOUNDING FATHER
According to legend, Vanderbilt devised contract bridge on an ocean liner travelling from Los Angeles to Havana.

ELY CULBERTSON
A flamboyant American of Russian origin, Ely Culbertson put bridge on the map in the 1930s by organizing high-profile challenge matches. He also published popular books on contract bridge.

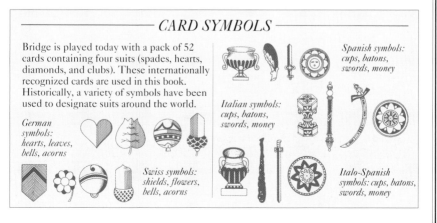

CARD SYMBOLS

Bridge is played today with a pack of 52 cards containing four suits (spades, hearts, diamonds, and clubs). These internationally recognized cards are used in this book. Historically, a variety of symbols have been used to designate suits around the world.

German symbols: hearts, leaves, bells, acorns

Swiss symbols: shields, flowers, bells, acorns

Italian symbols: cups, batons, swords, money

Spanish symbols: cups, batons, swords, money

Italo-Spanish symbols: cups, batons, swords, money

BIDDING SUMMARY

A table of the main bids in two popular natural bidding systems

•

THIS IS A SUMMARY of two widely played natural bidding systems, **Acol** and **Standard American**. Abbreviations used are HCP for high-card points, V for **vulnerable**, and NV for not vulnerable. In No Trumps bids the numbers refer to HCP; in other cases, to total points.

OPENING BIDS	STANDARD AMERICAN	ACOL
1. 1NT	16–18 HCP, **balanced** hand; 4-3-3-3, 4-4-3-2, or 5-3-3-2.	16–18 V / 12–14 NV; balanced hand.
2. 1♣ 1♦ 1♥ 1♠	13–21 points (including distribution). Long suit bid first: with 5-5 bid higher ranking, 4-4 lower ranking, suit.	13–20 points (including distribution).
3. 2NT	22–24 HCP, balanced.	20–22 HCP, balanced.
4. 2♣	Natural **game forcing** bid with a long club suit (5+ cards).	Artificial game-forcing bid: 23+ points or 9+ tricks.
2♦ 2♥ 2♠	**Game forcing**: 23+ points or 9+ tricks: minimum 5-card suit.	Forcing: 8 sure winners and 15+ points, 5+cards in suit bid.
5. 3♣ 3♦ 3♥ 3♠	**Pre-emptive bids**: 6–10 points, 7-card suit, no 4-card major. As a guide, your hand should be within 2 tricks of your bid if V, 3 tricks if NV.	
6. 3NT	25–26 HCP, balanced.	Solid 7-card minor suit (e.g. AKQJ987), 1 or 2 other high cards.
7. 4♣ 4♦ 4♥ 4♠	Stronger pre-emptive bids: typically 10+ points, 7- or 8-card suit. A V hand should be stronger than the NV as you lose more if **doubled**.	
VARIANTS 5 CARD MAJORS	1♥ or 1♠ require 5 cards; with 4-card major, bid 1♣ or 1♦ first.	Not part of original system, but now becoming more popular.
WEAK TWO BIDS	2♦, 2♥, 2♠ 8–12 points, 6-card suit; 2♣ now artificial, game-forcing.	Not in the original system; but popular with tournament players.
RESPONSES **1. To 1NT** IN SUIT	2♣ (Stayman) seeks 4-card major: 2♦, 2♥, 2♠ is weak hand, 5+card suit 3♣, 3♦, 3♥, 3♠ are forcing to **game**, with a minimum 5-card suit, 4♥, 4♠, 5♣, 5♦ plus any **slam** call are to play: opener should **pass**.	
NT RAISES	Balanced. 2NT, 8–9 HCP, invites game if opener maximum; 3NT, 10–14; 4NT 15–17; 6NT 16–18.	If V, same as Standard American. If NV, 2NT 11–12 points; 3NT 13–18; 4NT 19–21; 6NT 21–22.
2. To 1♣ 1♦ 1♥ 1♠	With 0–5 points, pass; with 6–10 choice is simple raise, new suit, or 1NT.	
SUIT RAISES	Immediate raises show four-card support. Point-count range: 1♥–2♥ shows 6–9; 1♥– 3♥ is 13–15; game forcing (Standard American), 10–12, not forcing (Acol). 1♥–4♥ (both systems) shows 8–12 HCP good distribution.	

NEW SUIT	A new suit at the 1 Level shows 6–18 points; at 2 Level 10+ points. 2♥ over 1♠ shows 5-card suit, all other suit bids may be 4 cards only. All bids in a new suit are forcing for 1 round (unless you passed before).
JUMP SHIFT	19+ points and game forcing. │ 16+ points and game forcing.
NT BIDS	1NT shows 6–10 points, no other bid available, may be unbalanced hand. 2NT 13–15 balanced. │ 2NT 11–12 balanced. 3NT 16–18 balanced. │ 3NT 13–15 balanced.
3. TO 2NT	3♣ seeks major suit: 3♦, 3♥, 3♠ are game-forcing (5-card suit minimum). 3NT/4♥, 4♠, 5♣, 5♦ and slam calls are to play there: 4NT invites slam.
4. TO 2 BIDS IF STRONG	2NT shows weakness (0–7 points); other bids show 8+ points, any new suit bid shows 5+ cards. │ 2♦ shows weakness (0–7points) after artificial 2♣; a new suit 9+ points, 5 cards; 2NT 8+ balanced.
IF WEAK	New suit is forcing. Raises may be real (strong hand) or pre-emptive. │ After strong 2♦,2♥,2♠, 2NT shows weakness; new suit is forcing.
5. TO 3 BIDS	**Responder** judges best contract on basis of 2 hands' **fit** plus strength. 3NT is to play; new suit is forcing, with a strong 5-card plus suit; raises to game may be strong (showing 4–5 tricks) or pre-emptive.
OVERCALLS 1. AT 1 LEVEL	1♦, 1♥, 1♠ overcalls show 8–16 points, and a fair to good 5-card suit. 1NT shows 16–18 points, balanced hand: in 4th position, 10–12 only.
2. AT 2 LEVEL	(If a simple **overcall**) it shows 11 points+, and a good 5-card suit. (If a **jump overcall**) usually 16–20 strong hand, good 5- or 6-card suit.
3. AT 3 LEVEL	(If a jump overcall) usually 16–20 strong hand, good 5–6-card suit. (If a double jump) often played as 8–12 pre-emptive bid, 7-card suit. N.B. jump overcalls are a matter of partnership agreement.
OPENERS REBID 1. IN NTs	1NT 13–15 HCP, balanced hand; 2NT 14–15 or 19–21 (if a jump rebid, e.g. 1♥-1♠-2NT). │ 1NT 13–15 V, 15–16 NV; 2NT (over 1 Level reply) 19–20 V, 17–18 NV; 3NT 18–20 V and NV.
2. IN OWN SUIT	Simple rebid (e.g. 1♥-2♣-2♥) shows 13–15 HCP, and a 5-card suit. Jump rebid (e.g. 1♥-2♣-3♥) promises 16+ points, and a 6-card suit.
3.RAISES	Simple raise (e.g. 1♥-1♠-2♠) 13–15, 4-card support (sometimes 3). Double raise (e.g. 1♥-1♠-3♠) 16–18, 4-card support, invites game. Game raise (e.g. 1♦-1♥-4♥) 19–21, strong 4-card trump support.
4. IN NEW SUIT	New suit at lowest level (e.g. 1♥-2♣-2♦) 13+ points, 2nd suit of 4+ cards. If a **jump** bid (e.g. 1♥-2♣-3♦), bid shows 17+ points, forcing to game. A **reverse** (e.g. 1♥-2♣-2♠), forcing partner to bid at the Three Level, shows 17+ points and guarantees 5 cards in first suit bid (hearts).
CONVENTIONS 1. STAYMAN	2♣ over 1NT asks for 4-card major suit: opener bids 2♦ if no major suit and 2♥ or 2♠ with 4 cards in that suit. With two 4-card majors bid 2♥ first.
2. BLACKWOOD	4NT asks for Aces. Standard responses are: 5♣ (0 or 4), 5♦ (1), 5♥ (2), 5♠ (3). 5NT after a Blackwoood 4NT asks for Kings on the same basis.
3. TAKE-OUT DOUBLE	This shows a hand you want to compete on. The main types are: (1) 13+ points, with support for 3 unbid suits, (2) 16+ points, a strong, 1 or 2 suited hand, (3) 19+ points, a strong, balanced hand.

GLOSSARY

Words in *italic* are glossary entries

A

• **Acol** A popular natural bidding system developed in the UK.
• **Auction** The sequence of bids leading to a final contract.
• **Away, To Lead** Leading high cards from a hand.

B

• **Balanced Hand** A hand with no *singleton* or *void*, and only one *doubleton*.
• **Block Suit** When the high cards in your hand prevent you taking all the winning cards from your partner's hand.

C

• **Cash** To play a winning card or cards.
• **Claiming** Claiming the contract as won without playing out all the cards.
• **Convention** An artificial bid or sequence of bids, which has a meaning other than the natural one. Examples in this book are Stayman and Blackwood.
• **Cross-ruff** Leading a card from one hand knowing there is a *void* in that suit in your partner's hand. Your partner then trumps the card you led and leads back *towards* your hand in a suit that you have no cards in. You then trump his card and lead back to him in the same way.
• **Cue Bid** A *forcing* bid in a suit the bidder does not wish to be trumps,

conveying to partner that he can win the first or second trick if the suit is led.

D

• **Discarding** Parting with a card (known as a discard), when you are unable to follow suit and cannot, or choose not, to trump.
• **Double/ Doubling** A bid that is made when the defenders believe their opponents cannot make their contract. If they succeed, their score is doubled.
• **Doubleton** A suit holding of two cards.
• **Drawing Trumps** Exhausting the trumps held by the opponents by leading the trump suit.
• **Duck** To play a low card in preference to a high one which could win the trick.

E

• **Entry** A card played to win a trick and transfer the lead to the opposite hand.

F

• **Finesse** An attempt to win a trick with a card lower than the opponents' highest.
• **Fit** Combined hand strength of eight or more cards in a suit.
• **Forcing Bid** Any bid that demands a further bid from your partner.

G

• **Game** A contract with a trick score of 100 points or more.
• **Game-forcing** A bid indicating that your partner cannot pass until *game* has been reached.

The Ace, King, and Queen are honours

H

• **High-low** Playing a high card, then a low card in a suit to show how many cards you hold or to ask for a further lead.
• **Holding-up** Declining to win a trick when you are able do so.
• **Honours** The top five cards in a suit: AKQJ10. Bonuses are given for holding honours on some hands: for example, if you hold four of the top five cards in a suit named as trumps in your hand, the bonus is 100 points. You also get a bonus for four Aces in No Trumps.

J

• **Jump Bid** Any bid made at a higher level than is necessary simply to make a valid bid.

L

• **Limit Bid** A bid showing the values of a hand within a narrow range.

O

• **Overcall** A bid that follows and outranks a bid by your opponents.
• **Overtake** To lead a high card, then overtake it with a higher card to gain *entry* into the other hand.
• **Overtrick** An extra trick, beyond the number you bid to make.

P

• **Part-score** A score below-the-line insufficient to complete *game*.
• **Pass** When a player chooses not to bid. If all four players pass, the cards are thrown in and dealt again.
• **Pre-emptive Bid** A high-level bid that denies the opponents room to bid at the lower levels.

R

• **Ragged Suit** A suit that has no cards in *sequence*.
• **Return** Leading a suit led by your partner at the previous trick
• **Reverse Bid** A bid that raises the *auction* higher than necessary, showing intermediate strength (17–18 points) eg 1♥, 1NT, 2♠.
• **Rubber** The best of three games.
• **Ruff** Another word for trump.

S

• **Safety Play** Playing a suit in such a way as to ensure your contract succeeds.
• **Sequence** A run of at least three cards (eg KQJ, J109). KQ10 and QJ9 are examples of broken sequences.
• **Signal** To give information about your hand through the cards you play.
• **Sign-off Bid** A bid which indicates that all values have already been shown.
• **Singleton** Only one card in a suit.
• **Slams** A *small slam* is a contract to make 12 tricks; a *grand slam* is a contract to make all 13 tricks.
• **Solid Suit** A suit where nearly all the cards are in *sequence*: eg AKQJ987.

• **Standard American** A bidding system that is widely played in North America.
• **Stopper** A card that will prevent your opponent winning a series of tricks in that particular suit.
• **Support** Your holding in the suit bid by your partner.

T

• **Take-out Double** A bid showing a hand with opening bid values and a desire to compete in the *auction*.
• **Tenace** Two *honour* cards not quite in sequence (eg AQ, KJ)
• **Through, To Lead** Leading through high cards held by the player beside you.
• **Touching** Cards of adjacent value in a sequence.
• **Towards, To Lead** Leading towards your partner's high cards.

U

• **Undertrick** A trick that leaves you short of your contract.
• **Unguarded** A suit in which you have no guard or *stoppers*.
• **Up To, To Lead** Leading to the second consecutive player's high cards.

V

• **Void** A suit in which no cards are held.
• **Vulnerable** A situation where penalties increase because one side has scored one *game* towards a *rubber*.

Discarding the ♠10

INDEX

GETTING IN TOUCH

BRITISH BRIDGE LEAGUE
13 Chaucer Road
Sudbury, Suffolk
Tel: 0787 881 920
The British Bridge League is a national
institution providing information about
bridge play and clubs in Britain. Within
the league, there are four national unions.

ENGLISH BRIDGE UNION
Tel: 0296 394 414
SCOTTISH BRIDGE UNION
Tel: 041 887 1903
WELSH BRIDGE UNION
Tel: 0222 611 652
NORTHERN IRISH BRIDGE UNION
Tel: 0232 668 279

ACKNOWLEDGMENTS

Jonathan Davis and Dorling Kindersley would like to thank the following
for their valuable help and expertise in the production of this book:

Matthew Ward and his assistants, Martin Breschinski, Christine Dormier, and
Chris Rennie, for photography at Plough Studios. Philip Gatward for additional
photography. Dawn Lane for make-up and props. Ross Opoczynska, Robert
Conway, Sami Sweeten, and Simon Murrell for modelling. Zia Mahmood for the
foreword. Irving Rose of the "TGRs" Club for the use of his club and his assistance.
Elizabeth Azis for the use of her specialized bridge equipment, David Westnedge
for supplying the many packs of cards, Chess and Bridge for the use of a bridge
table, Phoenix Hire for the chairs, and Yvonne Bisswell for making
the cloth used on the bridge table.

Maria D'Orsi for design assistance. Katriona John for research. Constance Novis for
Americanization. Martha Jaynes, Reg Grant, Susie Behar, Jane Laing, Jo Weeks,
and Laura Harper for additional material, extraordinary hard work, great patience,
and editorial assistance. Janos Marffy for the illustrations. Emma Boys for the Mac
artworks. Hilary Bird for the index. Lesley Riley for proof reading.

The following for additional photography: Culver Pictures p.63(bl). Mary Evans
Picture Library p.88(bl), p.89(tr). Hulton Deutsch Collection p.89(cr), p.17(br).
UPI/Bettmann p.89(cl), p.35(br). Picture research by Anna Lord.

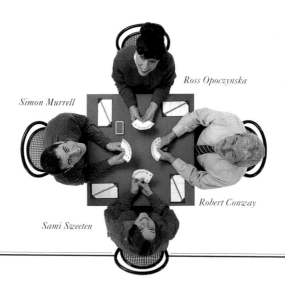

Ross Opoczynska

Simon Murrell

Robert Conway

Sami Sweeten